jewelry ON DISPLAY

Third Edition

by *MariAnn Coutchie*

ST Publications
Cincinnati, Ohio

Cover photo: Window for Little Lanes, Hazelton, Ont.; window design by Bob Sampson & Associates Ltd., Scarborough, Ont.; photography by Rob Gordon, Toronto.

Copyright © 1989 by Signs of the Times Publishing Co. All rights reserved.

No part of this book may be reproduced in any form or by any electronic or mechanical means including information storage and retrieval systems without permission from the publisher, except by a reviewer, who may quote passages in connection with a review.

Published by ST Publications
407 Gilbert Avenue
Cincinnati, Ohio 45202
U.S.A. 513-421-2050

Staff of ST Publications:

Publisher	Jerry R. Swormstedt
Project Director	Carole Singleton Emery
Project Editor	Laurel A. Harper
Art Director	Laura Baron-Stull
Asst. Art Director	Deborah Vatter
Typesetting	Diana Shelton, Janet Roberts

Printed in the United States of America

Jewelry On Display, Third Edition
ISBN: 0-911380-82-5

Library of Congress Cataloging-in-Publication Data

Coutchie, MariAnn.
    Jewelry on Display / MariAnn Coutchie. — 3rd ed.
       p.   cm.

    Includes index.
    ISBN 0-911380-82-5
      1. Display of merchandise. 2. Jewelry trade. I. Title.
HF5849.J6C68 1989
659.1'96882—dc19
                                      88-31428
                                        CIP

dedication

To all those who think of jewelry as the symbol of love, and are motivated to project an image befitting this symbol.

contents

Introduction 1

Chapter 1   *Composition* 3

Chapter 2   *Color* 9

Chapter 3   *Lighting* 17

Chapter 4   *Presentation Displayers* 25

Chapter 5   *Signage* 31

Chapter 6   *The Window* 37

Chapter 7   *Themes* 41

Chapter 8   *Installing Displays* 47

Chapter 9   *Special Promotions* 53

Chapter 10 *Christmas* 59

Chapter 11 *Displaying Diamonds* 63

Chapter 12 *Displaying Watches* 67

Chapter 13 *Store Planning* 71

Chapter 14 *Security Tips* 79

Chapter 15 *Photographing Your Window* 83

Glossary 89

Appendix: *Materials Sourcelist* 93

Index 105

introduction

Good displays don't just happen. They result from a sound knowledge of composition and color.

Photo courtesy of Chippenbook

Every facet of your jewelry business can become a tool to increase sales volume. By the way the phone is answered and customers are greeted, prestige is established. Information relayed to customers about jewelry sells product knowledge — and establishes credibility for the business. The image conveyed through windows, the store interior, indeed the whole building, sums up what your business has to offer the public. Those who neglect **display** are overlooking one of the most powerful sales tools available.

To put display to work effectively, you must first understand exactly what it is. Display is the art of presenting merchandise using fresh new concepts of old ideas. Good displays catch consumers' eyes and plant seeds of desire that often bloom into sales. Display people are artists, salespeople — **visual merchandisers.**

But good displays don't just happen. The successful visual merchandiser's abilities are based on a sound knowledge of composition and color, as well as dedication to the meticulous preparation of merchandise. These talents can be vital assets in promoting and marketing jewelry.

Display should help build a store's prestige and lead to increased sales. Additionally, it can inform viewers — for example, show them proper fashion accessories, the birthstone of the month or new jewelry concepts. Display relates a picture of beauty or evokes a sense of curiosity in all who view the store's window. In essence, display is a form of commercial art.

If you're not yet convinced that good presentation is worth your time and effort, consider this: Sixty percent of all buying is done on impulse, according to the Point-of-Purchase Advertising Institute. This fact alone establishes a major challenge for retailers to create displays that inspire and captivate their audiences. Visual merchandisers, more so than anyone else, can open this door to increased sales. They create a welcome image, establish markets for merchants and relay the philosophy of the store. They are key to the success of any retail business.

The object of this book, then, is to set forth presentation fundamentals as well as supply information on display's role in jewelry retailing. An innovative image is exciting by its very nature. It demands attention and action, and creates the desire to identify with that image — ideally through purchasing the merchandise shown. Therefore, exploiting display knowledge can benefit both retailers and the economic life of the jewelry industry. Windows are eyes into the store, the first encounter passersby have with your business. Progressive merchants exploit their windows for display and profit. They harness this force, put into motion by creative images, to generate more sales.

Displays that stress merchandise alone are things of the past. Display is of little value if it doesn't accomplish these goals:

- Promote products.
- Educate customers about your products.
- Convince the public of the merits of buying your services and products.
- Publicize your business, and build prestige.
- Lay foundations for future sales.
- Show community support.

Study these objectives of creative, successful displays. Then strive to develop your own that will stir the imagination and curiosity of passersby — and make them loyal customers.

Chapter One

composition

"Webster's Dictionary" defines **composition** as "arrangement into proportions or relations; into an artistic form, a work of art whose elements are combined artistically." In display, composition is the way merchandise is arranged in interior or window displays. Think of it as a three-dimensional picture. In our case, the subject of this picture is jewelry, arranged not only in a pleasing design but one where each piece of jewelry is seen at its best, making it easy for viewers to identify with.

Good composition starts with the correct division of areas of a window in relation to merchandise and props. All are significant parts of the total window image. Each jewelry item should be harmonious with the whole window display and contribute to its purpose, yet retain its individuality.

How the display is composed depends on the idea or theme, the manner in which the merchandise is stressed, color palette, and the angles and intensity of lighting. Also, the placement of merchandise relative to its height, width and depth to create a feeling of pleasing proportions is vital to a well-composed setting. All these facets of composition are significant, each part of a larger picture.

Be sure symmetrical compositions aren't too conventional, or the results could lack vibrance. This window injects an element of surprise — most effectively spotlighting the merchandise. (Window for Z.C.M.I.: Scott Morehouse, designer; Ron Nelson, director)

Asymmetric compositions consist of three-part groupings, with jewelry placed at the focal point for emphasis.

Composition is not based merely on a set of restricting rules. It is deeply ingrained in nature. All matter has in its form a rhythm and unity related to the whole. If there is a breakdown in this order, chaos normally results. Therefore, it only makes sense for anyone involved in display to understand the types of composition for a foundation on which to compose windows.

4

There are two basic types of composition: **symmetrical** and **asymmetrical.** Symmetrical compositions have balanced proportions of size and shape, and relative positioning of parts on opposite sides — such as rows of jewelry lined up equidistance from each other. No one piece stands out; they are a mass grouping. Symmetrical compositions are viewed as a whole; individuality is lost in the mass.

The nearer these visual forms are to each other, the more likely they are to be seen as a single unit. For this reason, symmetry is often used to display volume-produced items during a sale. This is particularly effective when there are many items in a limited choice of styles, and the price is reduced. Jewelers frequently use symmetrical composition to promote watches.

Symmetrical composition can relate a sense of dignity. The effect is poised and passive, rather than stimulating. Symmetrical compositions may be used effectively in moderation if an empty spot is allowed between each unit. This helps to overcome the feeling of mass merchandising.

Symmetrical composition is easily executed, but a word of caution: If only the conventional rules of symmetrical composition are followed, the results could lack vibrance. Passersby will see only a mass of jewelry rather than individual pieces. The situation is much like viewing a field of wild flowers from a passing car — there's no opportunity to inspect a particular flower. It's very difficult to stop busy people on the move with this form of composition unless they are actually shopping for jewelry. Use symmetrical composition wisely or it discourages, rather than encourages, customers from entering the store. Remember the following about symmetrical composition:

- It's effective for mass promotion.
- It can imply a special sale.
- It has formal balance, lending a sense of dignity.
- The nearer visual elements are to each other, the more they are visually grouped as a unit.
- Allow an empty space between each unit to be effective for general display purposes.

Asymmetry
The other basic form of composition is asymmetric, founded upon a three-part grouping such as that of a triangle. In a jewelry display, the main piece should have the greatest or tallest mass so that it dominates the arrangement. Place it slightly above center of the window area, either to the right or left. This is the beginning point of your triangular composition. Visually this is the most important position in the window area, the center of interest and starting point of the eye pattern. It is called the **focal point.**

The effects of a basically good display can be lost if the composition is divided so that the background overpowers the jewelry.

Each successful sales-oriented window has a focal point. The rest of the window display should emphasize merchandise placed here. This focal group dominates the display by its location, size and importance. It should have proportion and balance within the group itself, as well as in relation to its surroundings. The second-most important spot — the **intermediate** position — may be either to the right or left of the focal point. The **subordinate** position should be placed opposite the intermediate, completing the three points of the visual triangle.

Height and width can also be asymmetric. Proportions of the display units are established by the relationship of the units to the area bound by the window base (flooring). The top is bound by the top of the display case or the first dominant horizontal line if the window is draped, and the sides are bound by the nearest vertical line, or wall.

To establish the maximum height of the window, visually divide the height in half. The tallest line, called the **height point,** should extend slightly above center of this line. If the tallest line is too high or on the visual center of the window wall, it divides the window into uninteresting areas and/or the background is more dominant than the merchandise. On the other hand, if the line is too low, the upper wall area becomes overpowering.

Be careful to not overwhelm viewers with too much merchandise in the windows; rather than entice customers into the store, the display might connote chaos.

Featured jewelry should be placed along the path of the tallest line, slightly above its visual center. Use displayers or place the jewelry on background material that reaches to this height. The unit's width should not be greater than its highest visual line; therefore, height is the guide for the width of a unit.

Remember these rules when planning an asymmetrical composition:

- It has three parts, as in a triangle.
- The focal point is slightly above center and either to the right or left of a given area, dominant in height and width placement. It is the starting point of the eye pattern.
- The intermediate position (second in importance) is placed on either the right or left side of the focal point, at about two-thirds of the focal point's height.
- The third position — the subordinate — is placed opposite the intermediate, at about two-thirds the intermediate's height.

To create an asymmetrical window composition, first visually divide the whole window area into a triangle, with a focal point and intermediate and subordinate areas. Width of these units should be about two-thirds of the entire designated area. Establish the proper height for your display by using the rules previously given. Also, remember that if the units are to be viewed separately, the space between each should be greater than the units' widths. But, if the units are to be viewed as a group, the space between each should be less than their width. Smaller units may be added in such a manner that they do not dominate.

Empty space is also an important part of a window composition. This space has great value because it allows room for "visual breathing." It also allows time to develop a point of understanding, a place to stop thoughts and start to identify with the merchandise.

To sum up, remember that composition is the foundation of display. It can be either symmetric or asymmetric. Paint symmetric as poised and passive, asymmetric as vibrant, exciting and innovative. No matter which is used, give it room to properly express the message.

Chapter Two

color

From prehistoric times, humans have had an innate desire to express their feelings, thoughts and needs through color. As early as 15,000 B.C., cave dwellers used color to create murals showing scenes from their daily lives. Greek philosopher Aristotle realized that to have color, we need light, and that different materials absorb light in different ways, resulting in different colors. This theory still stands.

Isaac Newton is credited with discovering the color spectrum. While experimenting with sunlight passing through a small opening into a dark chamber and falling on a glass prism, Newton discovered the light beam broke into red, orange, yellow, green, blue, indigo and violet. Although the spectrum ran in a straight band from red to violet, Newton twisted it into a circle and, thus, developed the first **color wheel.**

J.C. LeBlon discovered the primary nature of red, yellow and blue in pigment mixtures. **Primary colors** are the three basic colors that cannot themselves be created by mixing any other existing hues, but from which all other colors are produced.

Today, comprehensive standards establish colors in terms of hue, value and chroma. It is interesting to know some background on a subject and you may wish to delve further, but our main interest here is how to use color to sell merchandise.

People naturally tend toward order and prefer color harmony based on an orderly plan. Even the untrained eye is capable of instinctively discerning whether two colors clash. People are attuned to natural world surroundings, where colors are seldom seen in full intensity. When intense hues do occur, they are in small amounts. The sky is usually a soft blue; spring greens are soft, grayed yellow-greens; and fall and winter browns are mellow brown-reds, green and yellow-browns. Many people, therefore, find man-made colors harsh, loud and clashing.

Color stirs deeply ingrained reactions. In a broad sense, colors are divided into two categories: **warm** and **cool.** Warm hues — red, orange, yellow and their variations — are associated with the sun. Cool hues — green, blue, violet and their variations — are the colors that appear as the sun goes below the horizon, or in shaded areas. Therefore, we associate warm colors with action and vitality, while cool colors are considered sedate.

The facts and guidelines of color usage related here will be based on the primary colors of the **Grumbacher color computer** (a color wheel). Purchase it in any art supply house or large stationery store, and place it in an accessible spot for easy reference.

As already stated, the three primary colors — red, yellow and blue — are most important of all, combining to form every other color. Mixing two primary colors forms a **secondary color.** For example, combining primary yellow and red results in the secondary hue, orange. If one primary is dominant (caused by using a greater amount of this color), the result is a hue tending toward that dominant primary. In a red/yellow combination, adding a greater amount of yellow results in yellow-orange; red-orange is formed when more red is used. The same holds true for blue and red: Violet is the secondary color that results, but if more blue than red is used, blue-violet is formed; if more red is added, red-violet results.

Now, turn around to the other side of the color wheel — the cool side. Find the secondary hues made by combining yellow and blue: yellow-green, green and blue-green. Again, depending upon which primary dominates, the secondary will tend toward the yellow or blue.

Intermediate hues are a combination of primary and secondary colors. They have compound names such as yellow-green, which is a mixture of primary yellow and secondary green. Understanding the origin of a hue enables one to describe the color by its proper name, and vice versa.

Two colors are **complementary** if they turn into white light when passed through a glass prism. Complementary hues are contrasting colors that lie across from each other on the color wheel. The line used to connect the two is drawn through the center of the circle to the opposite side — the circle's diameter. Colors always

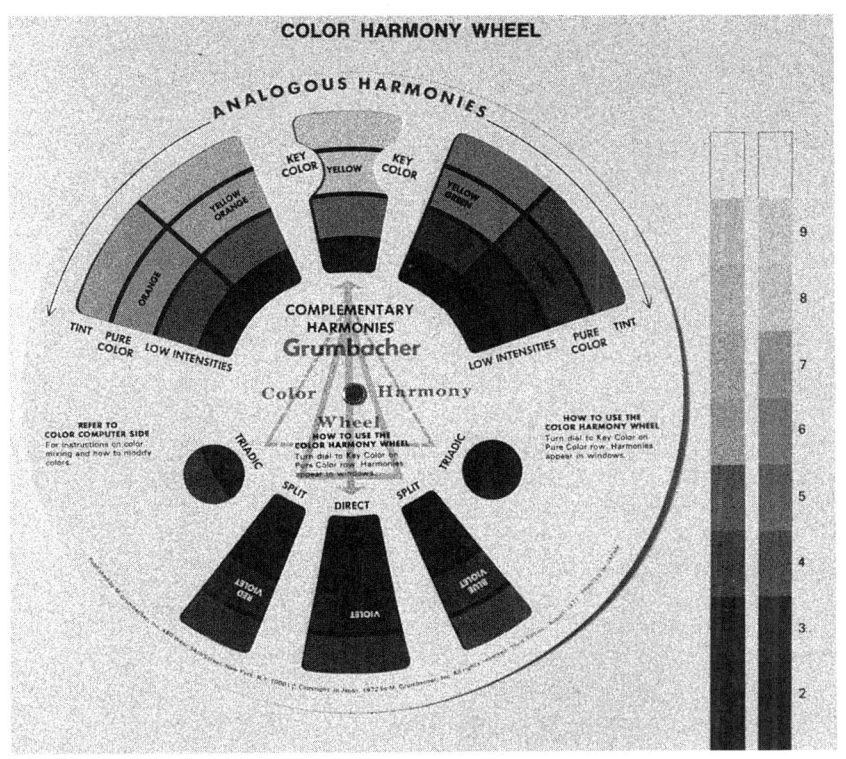

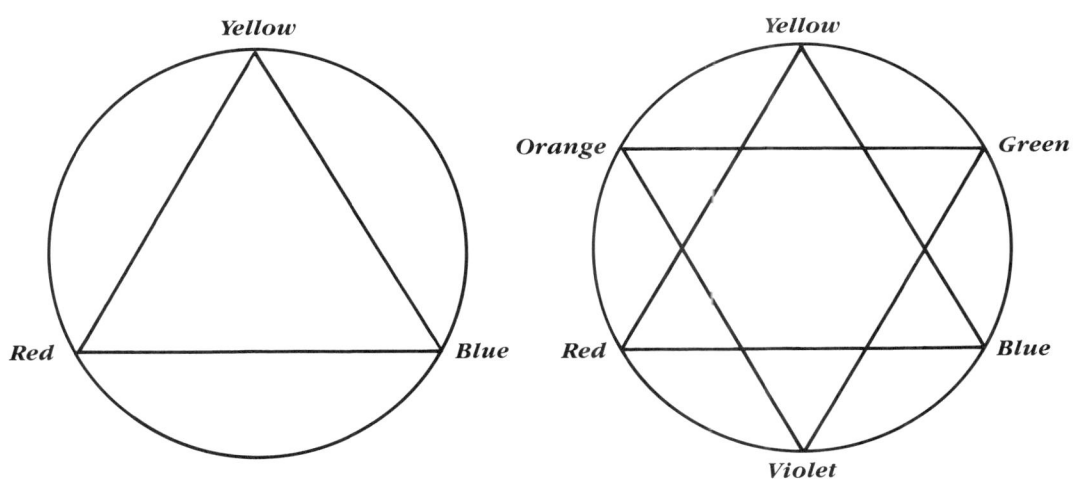

have greater visibility and are more compelling when placed next to their complements. Also, when a color is used with its complementary hue, the preference rating usually rises.

The quantity of the complement is important. Sometimes it's far too vibrant and should be diluted. This can be accomplished by adding white to create a lighter tint, or diluting it with black for a darker tone. Add its complement and the hue becomes grayed. The amount of dilution is determined by individual preference. Dilution does not change the complementary relationship of the colors.

Complementary colors are important in display, producing a psychological balance of warmth and coolness. Also, colored stones appear more intense when placed against their complementary colors. For instance, rubies set on green pads look more intensely red, while the green pads appear greener. Or place apple-green jade on violet ribbon — the intensity of the jade is greatly enhanced by the violet background. But choose the violet shade with discretion.

Analogous hues lie next to or near each other on the color wheel, sharing a common color. They provide little visual contrast and lack variety as to their psychological effect. Analogous colors are either both warm or both cool, while complementary colors always include one warm and one cool.

Tints are made by adding white to a hue, **tones** by adding black and **shades** result when the color's complement or gray is added. These facts can be applied to create color schemes that enhance the beauty of jewelry and increase sales.

When a third color is introduced into a display, it should generally be a tint or tone of one of the two hues already in the scheme. If the color scheme is pink (red plus white) with green accents, the third color should either be a tone of red or a tint of green. To increase the stimulating effect, a small amount of pure red pigment can be added; to soften a brilliant green, introduce a green tint.

After becoming familiarized with the basic color premises, start applying them to display. The first step toward using color to full advantage in presentation is to audit the colors of the fashion season. What hues are big news now? Good sources for the answer are fashion magazines, such as ***Vogue, Harper's Bazaar*** and ***Seventeen.*** After determining these colors, refer to the color wheel to pinpoint specific color harmony combinations. The wheel can also be a tool to help picture these hot fashion colors in changed intensities and values.

Borrow proven schemes from the windows of others, or use the colors of nature to please spectators. Color photographs or artwork, magazine advertisements, colored stone combinations, or any other colorful object can be used in your windows to increase sales.

There are no strict rules for color, and nature is whimsical with its usage; therefore, depend upon the color wheel as a guide. Feel free to alter or rearrange color to suit your purpose or fancy, but do so with caution. The more color is used, the simpler it becomes to choose palettes that stimulate sales.

The following color schemes work well in windows:

- **Monotone settings** use only one color, such as blue flooring, displayers and background. Monotones don't excite or draw attention, but if used in front of contrasting or complementary backgrounds can be very dramatic. Picture a string of pearls displayed in this way.
- A **monochromatic scheme** consists of any desired value and intensity of a single hue, such as red, hot pink and light pink used in a Mother's Day window. All are derived from the single color red. Wonderful effects can be achieved with one color. Monochromatic arrangements placed against contrasting backgrounds capture attention. Placing merchandise against one of the color values in the monochromatic scheme creates a subtle relationship with the background. Against a complementary background, a monochromatic arrangement becomes brilliant. Against any other color background, however, it is discordant.
- An **analogous scheme** is made up of adjoining or adjacent colors on the color wheel. Start with yellow (or blue or red) and note that yellow-orange and yellow-green, consisting mostly of yellow, are very close in relationship. These three form a close analogous affiliation in both intensity and value, and are almost certain to be harmonious. This scheme has a clear indication of mutual proximity, with pleasing results. Generally, use a primary or green as the center of an analogous scheme.

    Since analogous colors are in close harmony, they may tend to be monotonous. However, they can be made more interesting by placing emphasis on one hue in the group. This color can be made dominant by using it over a larger area than the other two colors, by placing the darker hue in the group against the lighter hues, or by being more intense than any other in the scheme.
- **Analogous with a complementary accent** is a combination of two analogous colors. The accent is introduced with a small, intense complement of one of the two colors. Such accents, particularly if brilliant, often have a power much greater than expected. This touch can give surprising life to the whole window. For example, in a yellow, yellow-green and blue-violet color setting, the featured merchandise should be placed in the blue-violet area.
- **Complementary color schemes** are created when colors directly opposite one another on the color wheel are used. Despite the fact colors that are called complements are different in most respects, remember that a definite relationship exists between them. They include one warm and one cool color. They are optically, psychologically, and physiologically balanced. Yellow-green

and red-violet, for example, are as different as any two colors could possibly be; but they are subtly related, as the word "complement" implies. (Black's complement is white. When using black in a setting, remember that it's a negative color and balance it with a positive, warm hue.)

When properly handled, complements can result in very pleasing color harmonies. Most people seem to prefer contrasting harmonies over analogous ones. But control these contrasts or chaos could occur. Generally, let one of the two complements be dominant in area and strength; otherwise, the selling impact is lost and the color scheme upstages merchandise. Remember, a colored stone always tends to look more intense on its complement. This fact is particularly important when showing stones to a customer.

- **Near-complementary color schemes** use complements that aren't true complements, but rather near to the true complement on the color wheel. This information is useful when it's difficult to find complementary colors in the same material, such as fabric for pads. Complements that are approximate are pleasing. The complement of red may be either blue-green or yellow-green. This is called a **split complement,** since the colors are split on the color wheel by the true complement, green.
- A **triadic harmony** is shown on the color wheel as a complementary pair, plus a third color. The triad may come from either side of the color wheel. For example, if using yellow, red-violet and green, let one be dominant and the other two a tone, tint or shade of their color. Also, let one dominate in area, one be intermediate and the other subordinate. Again, carefully consider the quantity and intensity of each color to be used in the window scheme.

Color is a powerful sales medium. Colors used in the window should be in line with consumer desires and relate to current market conditions. It's not a question of choosing a few shades by guesswork or hunch. Study market and consumer trends to assure that every color does something positive for stimulating sales. Let the color wheel be your initial guide. Color selection is a skill that should be developed, and like any other skill, the more it's used, the more it's fine-tuned.

Also, certain colors have symbolic meanings. Here are a few examples:

- Red is the color of blood, representing courage and sacrifice.
- Scarlet, or a red-orange hue of very high saturation, is a sign of dignity and rank.
- Gold, or yellow, means the sun, sun god and wealth. It may also represent cowardice, but usually relates to warmth and the wealth

of gold.
- Blue stands for sky, heaven and water.
- Green means hope, the color of spring and the renewal of life.
- Purple indicates rank and authority. The ancient expensive dye was derived from the purple fish, *purpura*. Purple robes were worn by Roman emperors and, later, by high-ranking prelates of the Christian church.
- Black represents death, the underworld, mourning, desolation.
- White means purity and chastity, but is also the color of mourning in the Far East and the color of surrender.
- Gray is colorless, figuratively as well as literally.

Jewelers are marketing a luxury product, so their windows should be lively and identified with fashion. Change each season with the fashions in a way that entertains customers. Move on with jewelry displays and bring them up-to-date to capture the market with color-excited sales. Look upon color as a tool, a medium that stimulates action and generates sales. Combine colors in a scheme that has meaning and relationship as to value and harmony.

Gone are the days when color was used merely for color's sake. Today, fashion and color knowledge dictate how to present and use hues. Explore the possibilities and employ color to its full potential in marketing your product.

Chapter Three

Lighting is one of display's most important tools, helping to create a store's personality and set moods. (Window for Cartier)

Photo: Matan Studio Inc., New York City

lighting

What merchandise customers see and how they see it depends upon the lighting. Light transmits the visual ability to evaluate color, shape and texture. It helps create a store's personality and puts shoppers in a buying mood. At the same time, light helps direct traffic flow and creates strategic points where salespeople can transact business with customers.

Consumers may become overwhelmed as they visually sort through a store full of merchandise. But aided by flexible lighting systems, you can single out items in specific presentations. A complex scene can feature display areas lighted to significantly brighter levels than their surroundings so they become easy-to-find oases for customers. Methodical shopping and the assurance of not missing anything on display are benefits of good lighting.

A lighting system's planning and flexibility are coordinated with the design and operation of the store. Plan lighting so it helps customers visually sort the merchandise and choose the areas they wish to shop in. Light should also be visually comforting and pleas-

Photo: Seiji Kakizaki, New York City

Track lighting offers the most flexibility in windows, easily positioned to enhance the visibility of merchandise. (Window for K. Mikimoto & Co.: K. Kawaguchi, designer)

ing. Points to consider in the planning stages include the size of the area to be illuminated and the ceiling height. Customer reaction shows that mood-elevating rooms almost always have some form of wall lighting or illuminated vertical surfaces. This is credited to the need to have boundaries of a space defined in some way. Vertically lit surfaces additionally help customers find wanted items and aid in creating circulation patterns throughout the store.

Another factor of lighting deals with the personal-scale relationship of customers to the store area. If the store is large, suspended light fixtures can render a feeling of shelter and create a more comfortable personal scale. This is why defined departments or shops within a large store are more pleasing to shop in.

Now consider the customers' seeing performance, or visual task. Visual task is determined by:

- Size — Often, quality is in small details, such as an intricate design on a charm. Distance is just as important as the actual size. Well-lit spaces enable customers to see effectively, at a distance of several feet, what kind of jewelry is within a case. This is vital to enticing impulse purchases.
- High or low contrast — A high-contrast visual task, such as a watch with black hands on a white dial, is easy to see. A low-contrast visual task, such as yellow-gold hands on a yellow-gold dial, is difficult to see.

Flexible lighting systems can be used to single out specific items in displays. (Window for Joseph Magnin Co., Inc.: Stan Steuart, director)

Photo: Davis, Mill Valley, Calif.

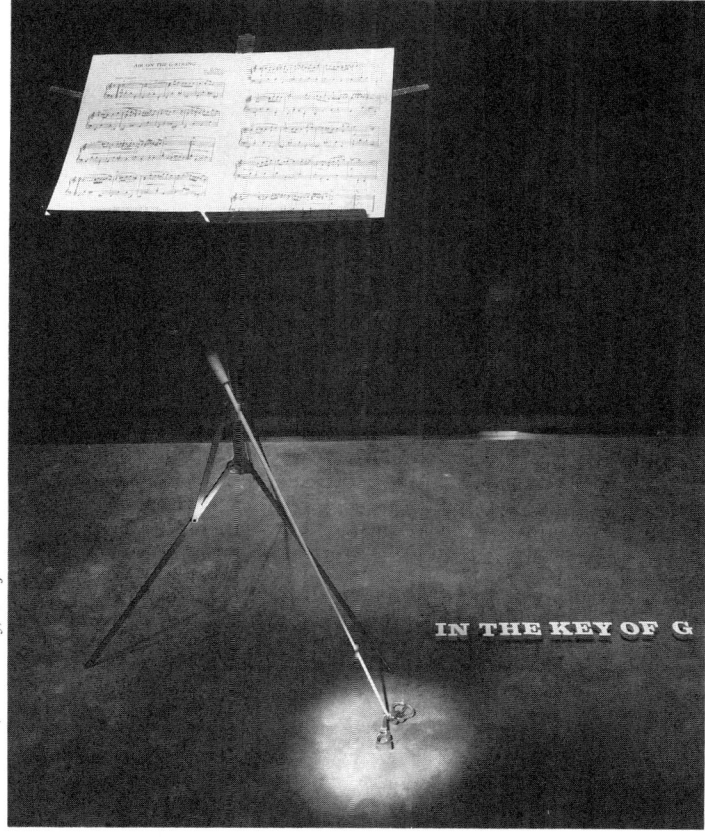

Inexpensive props and a single spotlight can create a simple, yet compelling jewelry display.

- Reflectance — Dark merchandise, such as oxidized gold or a matte finish on a ring's textured surface, is more difficult to see than a circular pin with a plain, buffed surface.

Based on these factors, then, be sure to consider the level of illumination needed to see small details and intricate designs in the merchandise. Also consider the variations in different metal textures and gems.

Within windows, track lighting offers the most flexibility. Spots may be added where needed, wallwashers may be used for back lighting that greatly enhances the visibility of the merchandise, and the addition of face lighting insures viewers don't miss any jewelry items shown. Light fixtures should be placed as near as possible to the front glass to illuminate the faces of the merchandise.

Very often during daylight hours, reflections on windows are so great customers cannot see merchandise in them. Adjust your lighting system to prevent this by increasing the illumination level. Light within the window must be greater than that outside in order to overcome the mirror effect of the glass. Add light adjacent to the inside glass so that it washes the glass with additional light and minimizes reflections.

The lighting system should also render a realistic color appearance. There are two general kinds of light: **warm light,** produced by incandescent lamps or flame sources, and **cool light,** such as natural daylight, produced by fluorescents. Warm lights tend to flatter, while cool lights are objective. The most desirable light source for diamonds and gems is a point source of light, with as near a daylight-simulating capability as possible.

Selecting light-source colors for store lighting usually involves three factors: efficiency of the source; **color-rendering** properties (how well the lamp presents the true colors of an object or environment); and the atmosphere produced by the source. Since these qualities are not available in one lamp, it is best to learn the characteristics of different lamps before making a selection.

A number of advances have been made in lighting equipment recently, particularly in the area of low-voltage lamps. Standard voltages are those used in most building applications — 120, 208, 277, 480, etc., up to 600 volts. Over 600 is classified high-voltage. Normal American household current is 120 volts, and most appliances and standard lighting fixtures are designed to run off this voltage. Any lamp below 50 volts is considered low-voltage, but the term usually refers to the very low end of the scale — 12, 9 or 6 volts, etc.

To better understand low-voltage, think of electricity as if it were water flowing through a pipe, then compare voltage to the pressure required to push the water through the pipe. High-voltage is like high pressure, and low-voltage is like low pressure. A valve is used to cut down the amount of water going from a large pipe into a smaller one; a transformer is used for the same purpose in the case of electricity. It may be a small transformer, just big enough for one fixture, or a larger, remotely located one capable of handling several fixtures at a time.

Until the last few years, the cost of low-voltage fixtures and transformers was higher than standard. But rising electricity rates have changed that. Low-voltage lighting is now popular for a number of reasons, foremost of which is its energy efficiency and, therefore, reduced operational costs. Low-voltage lamps can replace standard lamps up to two or three times their wattage, with the same light output. Reducing wattage up to 66 percent means a similar reduction in utility costs.

Auxiliary equipment in the total lighting system is similarly affected. For instance, smaller panel boards are needed with fewer circuit breakers and lighter gauge wire can be used, as well as smaller conduits and fewer switches. In addition, low-voltage lamps don't have the heat output of standard watt bulbs, so a savings in air-conditioning costs may also occur.

Along with their money-saving attributes, low-voltage lamps offer a number of other assets to jewelers. Their point source effectively shows scintillation in diamonds and penetrates the bodies of colored stones to enhance the hues. Another feature of low-voltage lamps is their size. Because they are smaller (some aperature diameters measure only 3/4 inch), the housing surrounding them may be smaller also.

Since low-voltage bulbs are smaller, their output may be controlled and directed more easily and accurately. Finally, low-voltage lamps are safer simply because of their low voltages, and the subsequent reduced risk of harmful electrical shocks.

Where may low-voltage fixtures be used? Anywhere track lighting or recessed accent lighting would be used, either commercially or residentially. In jewelry stores, they're good for making diamonds scintillate, or in any place where light needs to be projected or directed. Current trends suggest using low-voltage MR16, 50-watt lamps, spaced every 2 feet over showcases and positioned so that the light is directly above the leading edge of the case where the consumer stands. If mounted on a track, tilt the lamp at a 45-degree angle to the side of the showcase, parallel to the front edge so that light doesn't reflect in the consumer's or salesperson's eyes.

The MR16, 50-watt lamp is a down light that has a very small, powerful projection lamp with a dichroic reflector. This reflector is made from glass which has been coated with a special reflective-transmissive substance. The coating reflects all visible light, but allows infrared and ultraviolet rays to pass through the reflector. Over 60 percent of these rays are radiated out through the back

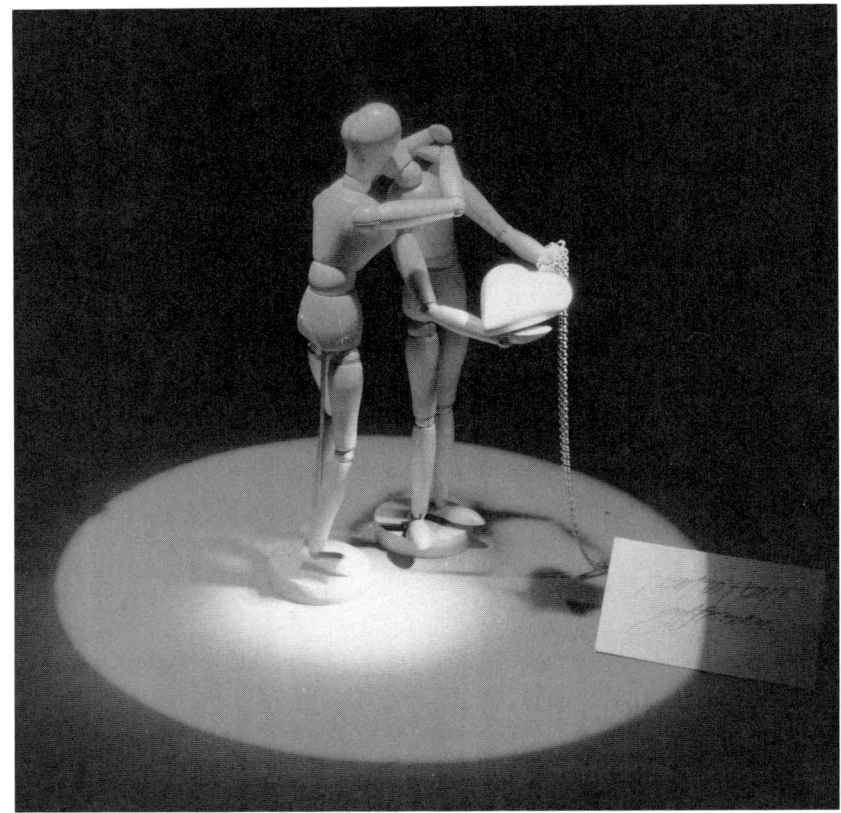

A simple setting can be transformed into a dramatic display via the correct use of lighting — in this case, a single spotlight. (Window for Z.C.M.I.: Mike Stephens, designer; Ron Nelson, director)

and sides of the lamp rather than forward with the light beam. The dichroic reflector, combined with a borosilicate glass lens in front of the lamp, removes approximately 99 percent of both the ultraviolet and infrared rays. This is a valuable asset for protecting heat-sensitive gems.

MR16, 50-watt lamps are tungsten halogen-cycle lamps, so they will not blacken during their life, and give virtually full light output to the end. These lamps provide very white light with color temperatures around 3,100 degrees K, so colors appear truer — a very important point where correct color rendition is necessary. The life of the bulb is from 2,000 to 3,000 hours.

Many fixtures are now on the market that house low-voltage lamps. They are designed with transformers that reduce 120 volts down to 12 volts, necessary for the MR16, 50-watt lamp to operate. The transformers may be built into individual light fixtures, or a remote, low-voltage transformer system may be installed. Remote transformers permit the design of extremely compact fixtures, because the transformers are located out of sight. But the transformer should be situated as close as possible (and local codes permit) to the light source since voltage might drop, depending on wire size and length of run on the secondary (low-voltage) side of the transformer. Investigate these through an electrical contractor.

Also on the market are retrofit fixtures with built-in transformers that screw into the regular light socket, enabling MR16, 50-watt lamps to be used in regular 120-volt sockets. One word of caution, however: Be sure the MR16s are used in porcelain light sockets only, as this fixture generates a lot of heat. While it's a good stopgap, it is better to use a regular fixture that's designed especially for low-voltage use.

Showcase interiors are typically lit with fluorescent bulbs. Now, however, there is a low-voltage, quartz halogen track light available that is whiter and brighter than fluorescent. This is especially excellent for diamonds and colored stones. The 1x1-inch track system uses 20-watt halogen lights spaced every foot. It has a remote, step-down tranformer and, therefore, plugs into any outlet.

Fluorescents are often used for general lighting in circulation areas, offices, work stations and gem laboratories. New fluorescent lights are constantly being developed that even more closely simulate natural daylight and reduce eye strain. The computer industry has brought this on, since glare, eye fatigue and vision blurring had to be overcome. Jewelers have benefitted from all this research, due to the development of a fluorescent that offers true color rendering for grading stones and less eye fatigue in working areas.

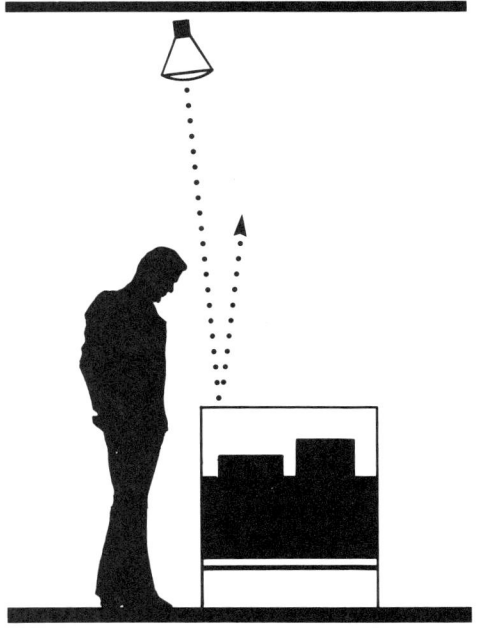

To avoid light reflecting into the customer's eyes, lamps mounted on tracks above showcases should be tilted at 45-degree angles.

To summarize, while fluorescents are good for work stations and general illumination, the best source of light for displaying diamonds, colored stones and metal jewelry is a point source such as only incandescents can offer. The low-voltage MR16, 50-watt lamp is the best on the market today, as it not only offers scintillation for the gems, but saves energy — something for which we should all be working.

So remember to explore the market thoroughly before settling on a system for your store. Be certain to select a flexible lighting system, then use it to its full potential and provide identification for shoppers, create an atmosphere that adds life to your store and directs scintillation to the gems. Light holds great potential for those who investigate all lamp qualities and apply them where they are most effective.

Chapter Four

Innovative retailers will find a whole world of displayers open to them, limited only by their imagination. (Window for Tiffany & Co.: Gene Moore, director)

presentation displayers

The forms on which jewelry is placed and held in position for viewing are called **presentation displayers.** They may be fabric covered, or made of wood, metal or plastic. Some are a combination of materials. But no matter what they're made of, displayers play vital roles in presenting jewelry. They provide a means of obtaining height in the window. They release merchandise from the total area of the window and allow it to be viewed individually. Displayers allow selective positioning in the window composition to show the jewelry items in their best light.

When selecting displayers, keep in mind that their height and mass should be determined by the window size. If a window is spacious, displayers should be higher; if it is deep, the displayers require greater mass. Place displayers in the window and look at them with a critical eye. Make certain they're correctly proportioned for the window. They should present jewelry near eye level, with various heights to individualize pieces shown and create interest.

Another thing to consider when selecting displayers is the type of merchandise being shown. The following suggestions are generally used in windows with ideal proportions (42 inches from the sidewalk to where the floor of the window begins; 18 to 30 inches high; 24 to 30 inches wide; and 14 to 20 inches deep):

A number of different types of jewelry displayers are available on the market today.

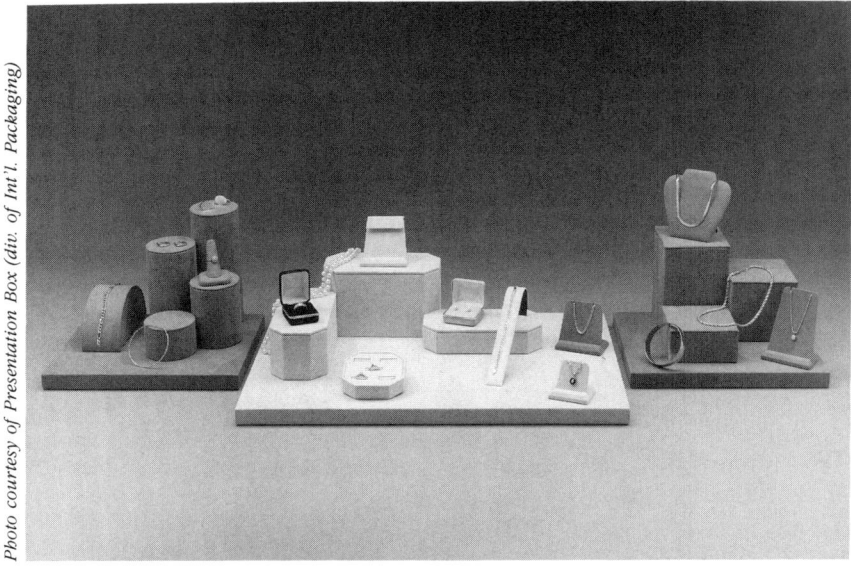

Photo courtesy of Presentation Box (div. of Int'l. Packaging)

Presentation displayers don't have to conform to normal standards in order to be effective.

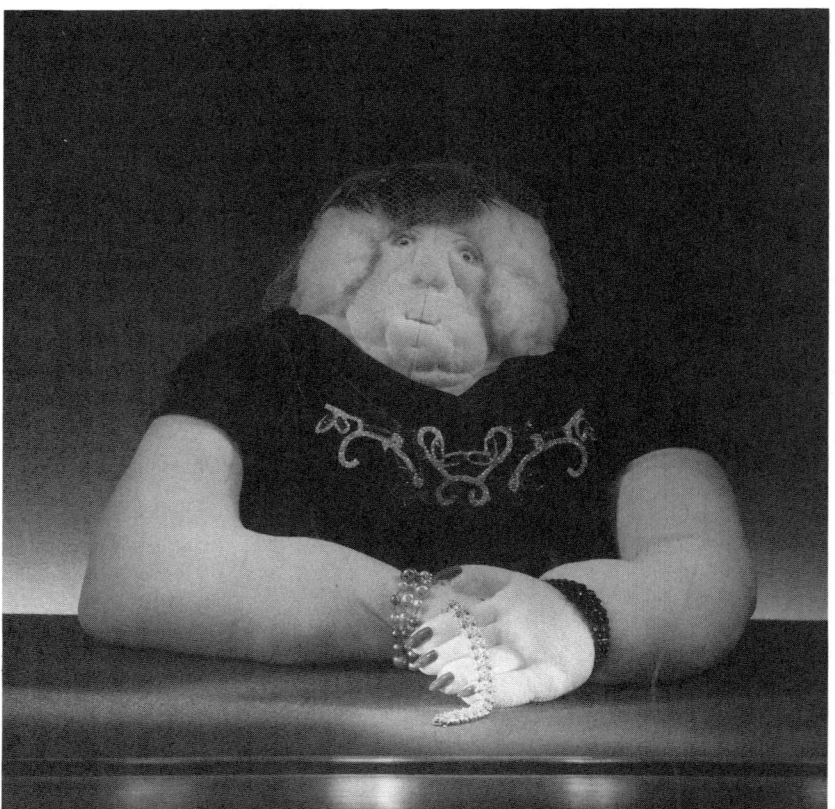

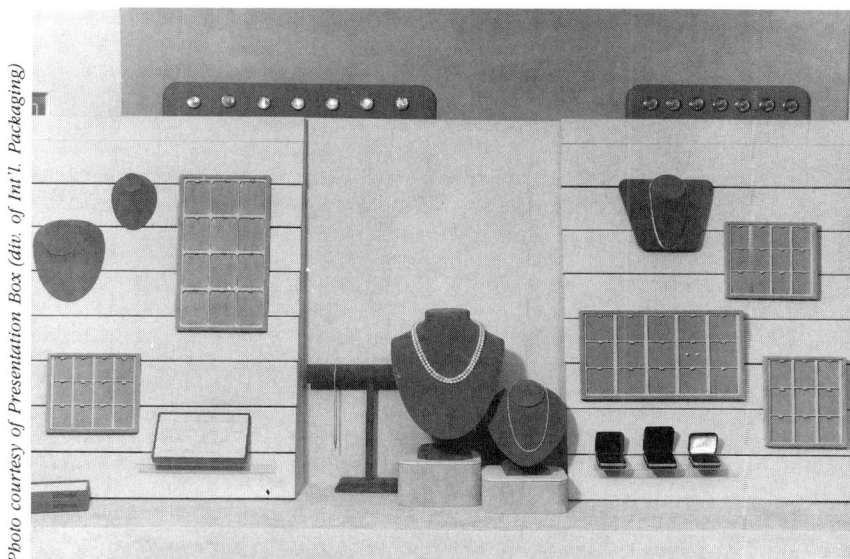

Photo courtesy of Presentation Box (div. of Int'l. Packaging)

When selecting displayers, consider the type of merchandise to be shown.

- Fabric-covered cylinders in sizes of 9 inches tall with a 6-inch diameter; 7 inches with a 4-inch diameter; 5 inches with a 4-inch diameter; and 2 inches with a 4-inch diameter. Do-it-yourselfers may want to purchase wallboard cylinders and cover them with fabric. Tops can be covered in fabric, glass or plastic. Good sources of uncovered cylinders are yardage, upholstering and floor-covering companies, where they're often free for the asking. For suggested sources of ready-made cylinders see Appendix.
- Cubes, in a variety of finishes, serve the same purpose as cylinders. Once again, these can be easily and inexpensively made, simply by cutting 2x2 or 4x4 pine lumber to various heights and gluing or nailing into cube shapes. Most lumber companies will cut to order for a small charge. Finish by sanding and spray painting in your choice of colors. (Matte paint seems to work best.) Or, use hardwood instead of pine and leave natural for a beautiful woodgrain displayer.
- Tables with removable pads make good displayers. Suggested sizes include 5x14x2 inches, 9x14x2 inches and 6x8x1 inches. Commercial display houses should have these in stock, or adapt a black, imitation-teakwood "chow" table, generally used for displaying artifacts. These are inexpensive and can be covered with pads, or the items can simply be placed on top the bare tables. If the tables become nicked or marred, touch up using black shoe dye. Most often, chow tables range from 4x5¾x1 inches to 6x7¾x1 inches in size. Occasionally, larger versions can be found. Look for them in Oriental gift shops.

Displayers should present jewelry near eye-level, with various heights to create interest and set off each piece. (Window for Zale Corp.: Art Smith and H. Neal Hay, designers)

- Another item from the Far East that adapts well to display is an Oriental wooden circular base. Made of black imitation teakwood, it's intended to hold a vase. For jewelry purposes, however, the base is excellent for setting off nice pins. Sizes normally range from 3- to 5-inch diameters, about 1½ inches high. Good sources, once again, are gift shops or wholesalers carrying Oriental lines.
- Fabric-covered ring displayers are musts for any jeweler. They come in finger-style or ring clips, available from various commercial display houses.
- Hands, from commercial display houses, are excellent for rings and bracelets and for lending height to displays.
- Pearls, beads and pendants are attractively shown on fabric-covered neck forms, also from commercial display houses.

There's really no limit to the shapes and items that can be used to effectively display jewelry. Mixing shapes can add an interesting twist to your windows. Slotted wall systems have become still another effective means for displaying within wall cases. As merchandise is changed, the wall unit can be altered to suit the new items. Most display houses offer these units.

Watch, cuff-link, upright strap-watch, bracelet, earring and easel-pin displayers, as well as earring trees and easels, are other types of presentation units put to good use by jewelry retailers.

Although the mounts and sizes of presentation displayers used in windows are determined by the merchandise, size and shape of the window, remember that the displayer's appearance is a definite factor in selling merchandise. Keep presentation units in good order by storing them in an area free from dust and unnecessary handling. Check them periodically to make certain they're clean and in good condition.

If velvet-covered displayers become matted, steaming the surface restores them. Hold the displayer over a tea kettle of boiling water and, with a soft paint brush or clothing brush, brush the velvet as the steam rolls over it. If the surface is soiled, dampen a clean white cloth with any good spot remover and rub gently until the surface is clean. If the spot fails to come out, discard the displayer.

Initially, displayers covered with various grades of suede are more expensive, but they take more handling, don't mat and offer a luxurious image.

Innovative retailers will find a whole new world of displayers open to them — for instance, children's wooden blocks, embroidery hoops inserted with fabric, wooden toothpick holders, natural-finished wooden egg cups filled with cork, even tree branches. Let your imagination evaluate every form and shape as to how it can become a fixture that will enhance the jewelry and present it in a matter that stimulates sales.

Chapter Five

signage

No window is ever considered at its full sales potential without an advertising message, designed to affect the buying behavior of passersby. In effect, this is point-of-purchase advertising. **Show cards** (or "readers") are written sales messages that reach consumers when they are at the location where the product is available for purchase; therefore, they can be very powerful sales catalysts.

A point-of-purchase show card gives concentrated information about the jewelry in the window. It is a means of stimulating sales, developing prestige, highlighting special promotions and harmonizing with a local or national advertising campaign. Show cards relay information to viewers without the necessity of salespeople. They act as mediators between merchandise and viewers, giving such facts as the name of the gem, if it's genuine or man-made, the carats or the price. They may even be fashion-oriented, e.g., "Diamonds & Spring Fashions Are Big News." In this instance, it's fashion news — even ego-directed, suggesting that if consumers are savvy about spring fashions, they'll be wearing diamonds. Show cards are a very effective means to enhance and give prestige to your store's image.

Information that should be on a typical show card includes the name of the store, type of jewelry or precious stone shown, where it may be found in the store, and price. Follow the window's theme

Though a picture is worth a thousand words, a few well-chosen words may help viewers to quickly comprehend the message of a display. (Window for Z.C.M.I.: Celeste Cecchini, designer; Ron Nelson, director)

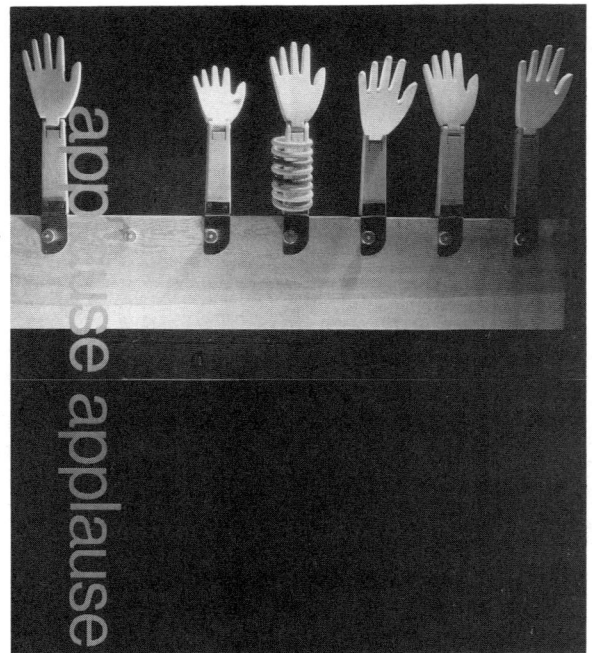

in the wording of the card. To assure viewers read this point-of-purchase message, it must be unusually interesting due to its novelty, rarity, ingenuity, product dramatization or some other important quality. For instance, start at the top of the card with the store name, and at the base list the department where the item can be found — "men's watch department." At the show card's center, state your message — "Give Him Read-Out Time." Be certain to include the price. The window setting might consist of ticker tapes and digital watches.

This tells the reason why ticker tapes are in the window. It may be considered a novelty interest, but it dramatizes the product and is what point-of-purchase advertising should be doing in windows.

It's essential that the card's message be brief, clear and to the point. It should be legible and distinct. The message should have a subject and predicate, but is best kept limited to about seven words. The type should be large enough to be read at a distance of at least 10 feet — 36-point type is good for this reason. (**Points** are the standard units of typeface measurement used by printers. One point is equal to about 1/72 inch, with 72 points equaling 0.996 inch.) Choose a typeface that's both readable and in keeping with the image you want to project. For example, bold letters are ideal for male-oriented windows, while brush script connotes a feminine image.

As already stated, show cards must be readily visible to quickly attract attention. The message may be printed on white or colored paper that is in harmony with the display. Some white drawing

Point-of-purchase messages can be auxiliary salespeople, introducing themes and suggesting an image with which viewers may identify.

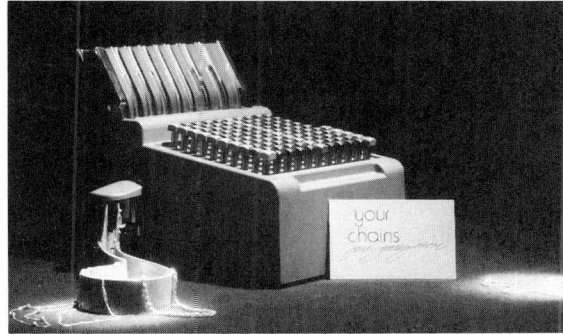

Show cards must be readily visible to quickly attract attention. (Window for Z.C.M.I.: Bob Coyle, designer; Ron Nelson, director)

Window messages act as liaisons between customers and salespeople, giving information about the jewelry shown and inviting customers inside to learn more. (Window for Wallach, New York

33

papers come spiral-bound in 6x8-inch sheets that can be cut to show card size. (Keep the small proportions of your merchandise in mind when deciding what size card to use. Normally, jewelry windows require either 4x5- or 5x7-inch cards.) Colored paper should be good, smooth-surface paper such as 240-pound cover stock. Any local art store should have a good selection. Also keep in mind the length of the message. Will it be a single- or three-line message? One-liners require long, narrow cards, while three-liners fit on smaller ones.

To prepare a sample show card with the three-line message "Gift Ideas for Your Love," first select the size of the letters. On the top line, "Gift Ideas," 36-point type is best. "For," on the second line, can be in lower-case, 24-point letters. The third line, "Your Love," repeats 36-point letters.

It is important to draw the reader's eye logically through the message. In this example, there are approximately 1¼ inches of letters, spaced 5 inches high. Since studies show that the focal point is slightly above and to one side of the card's center, the most important elements of the message should naturally be placed here. In our case, "Gift Ideas" is the point stressed; therefore, this line is set at the focal point. The second line is then centered below that, with distance between the two lines less than the largest letter's height. The third line is also centered, with the distance between it and the second line the same as that between the first and second. Draw light pencil lines for guides that can easily be erased when the sign is completed.

Study newspaper and magazine advertisements for good examples of layout. Notice how a "gaze-motion" pattern is employed to direct attention to specific elements. Here again, fundamentals of composition apply.

Once the location of the three lines has been established, pencil a small checkmark at the base of each line on either side of the card. These serve as horizontal guidelines. Next, place a check at the card's center, top and bottom. Work from the center out in both directions to assure equal margins.

Next, count the letters in each line, remembering to add one space between each word, then divide the total in half. For instance, in the first line, "Gift Ideas," an equal number of units are on either side, so the center falls in the space before "Ideas." Proceed as directed for line one with the remaining lines. Once the show card's line layout is established, the message is ready to be added.

Methods normally used to letter signs include hand-lettering, dry-pressure transfers and engraving. Many companies manufacture dry-pressure letter sheets in various typestyles that include upper and lower case as well as punctuation marks. Some also come in colors. These can be purchased either at a stationery store or art supply

Be certain the show card's message complements the merchandise.

shop. Dry-pressure letters transfer readily onto the card with a burnishing tool. (These are also available at the stationery or art supplier. It's important to use the proper burnisher to obtain the best possible results. Ask the salesperson for assistance if needed.)

Transfer the letters from the center out, in both directions. Hold the letter sheet firmly in place to prevent shifting. Position the letter in place on the card (front-side down) and, holding the burnisher like a pencil with the beveled edge down, simply trace over the letter with an even, moderate-pressure stroke. Note that as the letter is transferred to the card, its color changes from black to gray (or a lighter version of its original color). Keep going over it until the entire letter has changed color; otherwise, when the dry-pressure sheet is removed, part of the letter may cling to it. (If this happens, lightly tap the bungled character with the sticky side of a piece of masking tape until it lifts off.) Carefully pull the sheet away, then repeat the process for the next letter. To assure a more perfect adhesion, place a piece of paper over the character, then burnish again.

Another method of lettering — and one that's readily available to all jewelers — is engraving. The stylus (the cutting head of the engraver) can be adapted for lettering. Simply take it to a machine shop and have the head machined to a size that holds a ballpoint pen refill. Lay out the card just as for engraving, but transfer the ballpoint lettering onto it. This is a simple, quick method of executing cards for windows and store interiors.

Let your point-of-purchase message be an auxiliary salesperson. It can introduce a theme and suggest an image with which viewers may identify. It should be simple, but have an impact that will drive the message into action on sight. Lay it out with thought and care so that the merchandise and message complement each other. Remember to study sources of professional advertisements and keep good examples in an idea notebook for future reference.

Pay attention to not only the layouts in newspaper and magazine ads, but to their wording as well. Done by professionals, they offer a wealth of readable and effective information. As you become more proficient with spacing and wording, the task becomes quicker and easier.

Don't forget to price items. Contrary to what you might believe, it's surprising how many more sales are made when the price is shown upfront. Studies show that only about 3 percent of the population will buy first and ask the price later. For the other 97 percent, price is definitely a major factor in the purchasing decision.

Exterior signs

Windows and shop interiors aren't the only areas where signing is important. Exterior signs are vital to explaining who you are and what is being offered. Exterior signs say as much about the image of your shop as the interior decor and merchandise carried. So tie the sign into the shop's design, and keep the letter size and style compatible as well.

There are other points to remember. For instance, awnings have become very popular the past few years as an attractive means of signing. But did you know the awning material must be replaced every six years? And what about any legal sign codes in your area?

For this reason, licensed sign companies are good investments. They can offer designs and materials customized for the shop, and are familiar with any signing codes of the municipality or mall where you're located. Signs make a big statement about your store; therefore, be prepared to treat them with respect.

Exterior signs say as much about a store as the interior decor and merchandise.

Chapter Six

the window

Half a retailer's lease rate is based on the store's frontage. That puts a high cost-per-square-foot factor on the windows. Considering they are the most effective means of communicating with consumers and their cost to the retailer, it's important to use them to best advantage.

Architecturally, the window should complement the entire store image. Its design, including size, shape and form, should be compatible with the jewelry. Opening dimensions should ideally be 42 inches from the sidewalk to where the floor of the window begins; 18 to 30 inches high; 24 to 30 inches wide; and 14 to 20 inches deep. The width may vary, but visible height and depth should be adhered to because they are ideal dimensions for jewelry display and trimming ease. (The ceiling, however, may extend as high as necessary to house the lighting system from view, but the visible opening should not be greater than 18 to 30 inches high.)

Window lighting systems should be equipped for general overall illumination and accents, and flexible so they can be redirected for each display. Vent off heat by drilling holes in the ceiling if possible, or preferably air condition the window. Utilize theatrical lighting techniques, since good lighting effects gather an amazing amount of attention. Experiment with lighting the whole display and with lighting individual gems. Direct lighting on the star of the gem or jewelry being featured and note the various perceptions achieved as the lighting angles change.

For the front glass, a plastic-laminated security style is recommended, manufactured under the tradenames of Secur-lite glass, Vandal-Pruf, Lexan® MR-4000, Vigil Pane and others. Also, consider installing ornamental steel screens that drop in front of the windows at night to prevent breaking and entering.

Interior window walls may be drywall, plastic laminate (such as Formica®), painted or covered with fabric panels. The color choice is up to you, but keep in mind the decor of the store and make the palette unobtrusive as possible.

The floor of the window should consist of recoverable floorboards. The most suitable material for this is 1/4-inch Masonite®, which doesn't warp with heat. Available in most lumber yards, it can be cut to specification for a nominal charge.

To make the floor, begin by drawing a paper pattern of the window. Be sure each corner angle fits. Next, cut the pattern approximately 3/16 inch smaller all the way around; this allows for covering. Cut the Masonite® to size, assuring proper corner angles. Next, cut the fabric to size and use spray adhesive (the same type used for carpet and floor-tile bonding) to cover the flooring. Suitable fabric for the flooring includes felt, upholstery suede, drapery or dressmaking material.

If the window is elongated, divide the flooring into sections. The dividing line should lay in an area that will complement the general composition of the whole window. It is best to locate it where the composition of the display would normally be divided, between centers of interest.

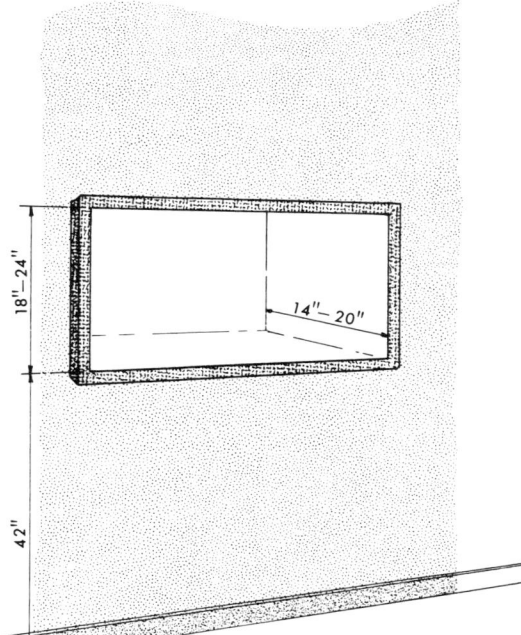

The ideal jewelry display window should be 42 inches from the sidewalk to where the floor of the window begins; 18 to 30 inches high; 24 to 30 inches wide; and 14 to 20 inches deep.

For inverted corners, spray adhesive on the edge of flooring. Cut toward the inverted corner, but stop the thickness of flooring from the corner. Using your thumbnail, push the fabric tightly into the corner, then miter as for regular corners.

Step-by-step instructions for covering the floor are:

- Place floorboard face down on the wrong side of the fabric.
- Cut fabric 3/4 inch larger than the floorboard. Note: If fabric has an up-and-down side, such as velvet, place the edge that will face the glass toward the same selvage edge for all pieces. (Selvage is the woven edge on the width of each side of the fabric.)
- Spray the adhesive from the edge of flooring to be covered, in a 1-inch strip on all four sides. Next, spray fabric from edge up to flooring. Do not get an excessive amount on the fabric, as it will bleed through and show on edges.
- Wait about 30 seconds and begin to cover.
- Pull opposite sides of fabric at the same time and press down gently. If there is a wrinkle, just pick up the edges, straighten and press down. Do this all around until fabric is smooth and tight, leaving corners for last.
- Pick up fabric at the tip of the corner and pull it gently but firmly over the corner of flooring. Press down. Note that there are two triangular pieces of fabric standing up on each side.
- Work the edges on each side of the corner smooth and tighten up to standing triangular pieces of fabric.
- Assuring the corner is wrinkle-free on the right side, cut triangles off even with the flooring.

For inverted corners, spray adhesive on the edge of the flooring also. Cut toward the inverted corner, but stop the thickness of the flooring from the inverted corner. Use your thumbnail to push the fabric tightly into the corner, then proceed to miter the two corners as described above.

Windows are the most effective means of communicating with passersby, so use them to best advantage.

If the floor is circular, proceed as with a rectangular floor, cutting fabric no more than 3/4 inch larger. Spray adhesive on the fabric and circle. Let stand 30 seconds and begin to bond. Bond opposite sides at the same time, pulling the fabric tight and wrinkle free. Work all around the circle. It will be necessary to part the bond from the circle to avoid pleating the edge, then rebond the smooth edge.

Ply ideas from set designers for window compositions, then scale them down to size. Strive to bring light where darkness was and add a sparkle of scintillation to the gems — but most of all, strive for beauty. The more you practice creativity, the greater your storehouse of ideas becomes. Constantly look, search, and sense every vision as to how it can become the theme for a window that sets new sales records.

Chapter Seven

Nearly everything seen or experienced can be transformed into a window theme. (Window for Bloomingdale's)

themes

Each display window should be built around a theme to be successfully sales-oriented. Themes are a very important facet of merchandising. A window without a theme is like a story without a plot, music without a melody or a painting without a subject. Themes are an intricate part of merchandising, suggesting how jewelry should be worn, but even more importantly, what it will do for the wearer's self-image. Themes are the means of relating merchandise to consumers in graphic forms that can be understood, remembered and identified with.

Jewelry is a commodity on the market that's considered 99-percent luxury. Its value comes through pride of possession, prestige and self-adornment. Jewelry also is a means of condensing an investment into a small, portable, negotiable object. In that sense, it has business value; but as a whole, it's considered pure luxury. Themes, then, captivate customers' thoughts and direct them to logical reasons for their purchases. For instance, what could be nicer than starting the New Year with a gift that expresses love — a garnet? The window theme would tell viewers that garnets are January's birthstone, demonstrate how lovely they are, show they come in many colors and that some are rare and, therefore, expensive.

Prop costs can be reduced by borrowing items from a neighboring store (such as in the case of this Valentine's Day teddy bear) and providing a courtesy card telling where they can be purchased.

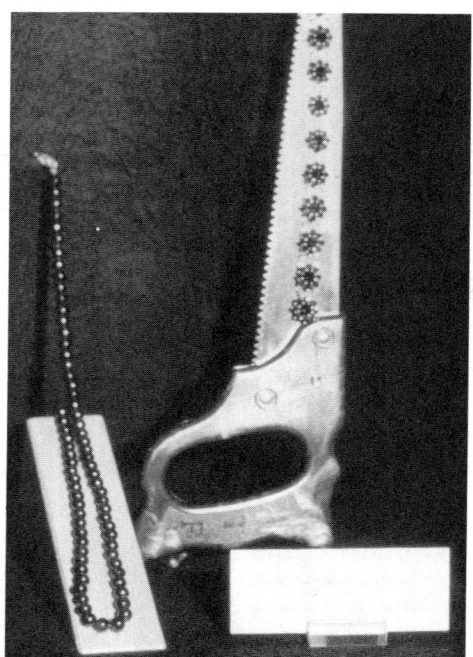

Startle viewers with displays using unusual combinations.

Clip out pictures from fashion magazines, then properly "accessorize" them with jewelry items.

Ideas for themes have many sources. They are stimulated by cultures, history, current events, modern enterprise and anything that stirs one of the senses. Fashion from the apparel industry is one of the best sources of ideas. Colors stressed in both men's and women's clothing are a great source: "Color It Emerald for Spring," or if you don't stock emeralds, "Color It Green for Spring." Show some green gems — jade, andradite garnet, green sapphire, peridot, diamond, chrysoprase, spinel, topaz, tourmaline, zircon and/or all the synthetics.

Holidays usher in all sorts of themes for window settings.

Jump on the fashion bandwagon and begin to pioneer fashions of your own. Stress the need for a jewelry wardrobe for each season. If fashion can sell the public on the idea, why can't the jewelry industry establish gems and metals for seasonal dress? Your only cost will be the effort expended to generate themes for display windows.

Clip out pictures of season fashions from major fashion magazines, then display jewelry that could be proper accessories. Don't neglect men's fashion. Men are wearing more and more jewelry, thanks to the clothing industry. This is a prime example of what an excellent advertising program the clothing industry has. They create markets and the jewelry industry can do the same with themes of fashionable adornment.

Nature is filled with themes. Its artistry excites the imagination with all its colors, shapes, seasons, beautiful birds, animals and minerals that could become display subjects. For instance, shells and sea life provide a handsome setting for men's underwater watches.

A theme can be whimsical, such as "Have a Heart of Gold. Give Her One." Borrow a teddy bear from a toy store for the setting. (Offer a courtesy card telling where the bear can be purchased. This helps defray costs, and gives additional exposure to the toy store.) Next, cover a heart in red for the background. Light beige makes a good floor color and sets off the intense red of the heart. Select heart-shaped jewelry and compose the window in a pleasing arrangement.

Various cultures offer a limitless supply of ideas. Customs and crafts of different ethnic groups stimulate interest and set the stage for featuring jewelry. Maps are colorful — pinpoint the source of various gemstones, showing the rough gem along with its cut and polished counterpart. "The World of Gemstones" makes a good theme. Remember to double-check the map locations for errors, which could spoil the impact of an otherwise artful display.

Historical themes are often used for anniversary promotions, portraying the past along with the present. Display a picture from your store's grand opening, then show advancements made in jewelry since that time. Themes also can be developed using famous historical settings or people. Honor our presidents by displaying jewelry for the Inaugural Ball (January 20) following an election. Or the theme could be "Election Is Over, But Diamonds Are In."

Every occasion, every event, every season will usher in themes for windows. These subjects are an intricate part of merchandising, since they give customers logical reasons for their purchases. Theme ideas geared to the months include:

- January's birthstone is garnet (as previously mentioned). Time is also a natural theme for this month, suggesting watch and clock promotions. January is also the traditional month for store-wide sales, and a good time to suggest jewelry appropriate for spring fashions.
- February's birthstone is amethyst. Valentine's Day and violets are traditional for this month, while presidents Lincoln and Washington are great for institutional promotions centered around "honesty," "integrity" and "character." Other February events worth noting include Groundhog's Day and the Mardi Gras.
- March's birthstone is aquamarine. Greenery and flowers are appropriate for St. Patrick's Day, and don't forget March 21 ushers in spring. Easter may also fall in March or April. Check the calendar.
- April is diamond month, so stress "the gift of love." Feature Easter, if it falls in this month. Even something as unappealing as income tax time can become a theme — suggest that refunds be used for a special jewelry gift, like a diamond. Spring house cleaning suggests restringing pearls or beads, redesigning gems from old settings by remounting or creating specially designed pieces.
- May's birthstone is emerald. Don't forget Mother's Day is the second Sunday. May is a great gift month, with lots of bridal showers and engagement parties, lending itself to every type of jewelry promotion imaginable. May flowers and baskets filled with jewelry make lovely windows. Also, Memorial Day is the last Monday of the month.
- June is the pearl month. It's the favorite time for weddings; school is out, so there are graduation ceremonies; Father's Day is celebrated on the third Sunday; and vacation time begins. Focus on watches for graduates, wedding gifts and pearls for the bride, and men's jewelry for Father's Day.
- July means rubies. Independence Day creates all sorts of patriotic themes, and it's also a month for vacation and travel.
- August's birthstone is peridot. Outdoor sports themes can be paired with sports watches in displays, while home entertaining

promotions can tout silver, china and crystal. Don't overlook back-to-school at the end of the month.
- September showcases sapphires. Fall jewelry accessories for upcoming holidays can be shown as well, along with back-to-college themes introducing watches, alarm clocks and school jewelry, such as charms, friendship rings and bracelets.
- October's birthstone is opal, those beautiful rainbow-of-color stones, along with tourmaline. Fall harvest, winter sports and Halloween trick-or-treat windows are appropriate now. Columbus Day is observed on the second Monday.
- November features topaz. Consider Thanksgiving and holiday-dining festivities. Demonstrate proper table settings and suggest table decorating ideas. The first Tuesday in the first full week of the month is Election Day; Veterans Day is November 11; and jewelry for the festive holiday parties taking place now is a must.
- December's birthstones are turquoise and zircon. This is the time for every type of jewelry to be featured for Christmas.

Along with themes for specific months, don't forget wedding anniversaries. The following is a customary gift list:

1st: Clocks
2nd: China
3rd: Crystal and glass
4th: Electrical appliances
5th: Silverware
6th: Wood
7th: Desk sets, pen and pencil sets
8th: Linen and lace
9th: Leather
10th: Diamonds
11th: Silver, gold, gold-filled and gold-plated fashion jewelry and accessories
12th: Pearls or colored stones
13th: Textiles and furs
14th: Gold jewelry
15th: Watches
16th: Silver holloware (sterling or plate)
17th: Furniture
18th: Porcelain
19th: Bronze
20th: Platinum
25th: Silver jubilee (sterling)
30th: Diamond
35th: Jade
40th: Ruby

45th: Sapphire
50th: Golden jubilee
60th: Diamond jubilee

The community calendar is also a great source of ideas. Check with the local chamber of commerce for dates of city events to feature in your windows. It's amazing how the shopping spirit of an area can be stimulated in this way. Remember, however, that your windows reflect upon the community's image, so keep them in good taste. Ultimately, of course, they reflect upon your store.

Begin to relate every event, season, nature, color, texture, art object, book — in short, everything you see or experience — as to how it can be transformed into a window setting. Accelerate your thinking in this direction, and it's amazing how many themes come forth.

Chapter Eight

installing displays

Window trimming requires organization, planning and meticulous preparation, all directed toward opening the door to more sales. Intense competition for consumer dollars means presentation has to be such that it holds the eyes and motivates a desire to own the jewelry. All this doesn't just happen — it takes work, time, thought and a budget.

The planning stage of a window determines the approach, reasoning and marketing of the featured product. Good planning should crystalize thoughts that lead to sales. First, consider what will be sold and advertised during the 10-day to two-week period a display is normally featured. Coordinating windows and advertising brings a greater return on invested dollars, since both support each other in relating the same message.

Advertising programs should help key the window image and, conversely, each campaign should be planned around the windows. Windows are, in effect, three-dimensional advertisements that place the product in front of consumers at the point where it can be purchased. Shoppers don't have to rely on adjectives to describe the product — the jewelry is right in front of their eyes where they can enjoy its beauty firsthand.

The next step in planning is to ascertain the reason for the display. Is it a sale window? Is it a promotion, intended to push a particular line? Maybe it's a gift window for Christmas, Mother's Day or Valentine's. Or is it directed solely toward prestige?

When in doubt about the amount of merchandise and background material to use in a display, follow this simple rule: Use less, not more. (Window for Tiffany & Co.: Gene Moore, director)

Each type of window calls for a specific kind of display. Gift and sale windows as a rule are trimmed more heavily. Prestige-building windows, however, direct consumers' thoughts to a few elegant pieces of jewelry, while promotional displays feature many styles of one particular object or line (for example, different styles of cuff links).

The amount of merchandise presented helps determine the size and style of background material. When in doubt as to the amount of merchandise and background material, follow this simple rule: Use less, not more.

In the third phase of the planning stage, consider the age group you want to attract. Is it the young, ready-to-marry group, or the business crowd? Is it the established middle-age group, the jet set, or average middle-class workers? The target audience determines how sophisticated the message and setting should be.

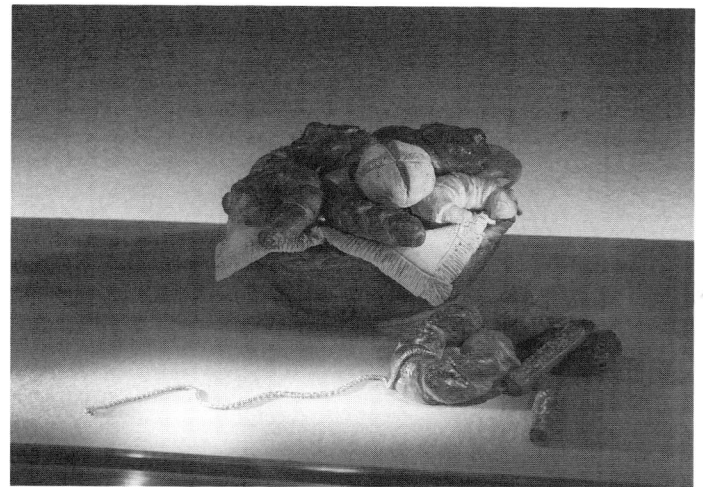

Any prop that sets the stage for the theme and shapes an image with which viewers can identify is appropriate for a window display.

Presentations must hold the eye and motivate a desire to own the jewelry. (Window for Barneys New York.)

During the planning process, also establish the size of the merchandise. Once this is done, determine the size and extent of the background material or embellishments to be in proper proportion to this merchandise. If the background material is too large, it overpowers the merchandise.

After the plans have been carefully formulated, begin preparing the setting. This involves taking the idea and developing it into the completed window. Once again, fashion magazines, an idea notebook and your own imagination should provide fodder for the window.

Begin by drawing a layout of the window composition. The plan can be small and simple. Draw the floor area and divide it, as described in the chapter on composition, into focal, intermediate and subordinate sections. Then divide each of these areas into thirds. Mark how to compose the window, using circles where each unit will be placed and sketch where the background will be located. This detailed preparation enables you to enter the window and quickly compose it.

Next, select and construct background decorations — maybe an artifact that lends elegance to the jewelry environment, wooden balusters for height, and platforms on which to place the merchandise. Any material that sets the stage of the theme and shapes an image with which consumers identify is appropriate.

What are some things to look for when collecting materials? The background should suggest an idea or theme that takes only a small amount of imagination to develop. Its height should complement the jewelry and be in correct proportion to the window size, and its color should complement the jewelry or be in harmony with it.

Each step in window construction should be carried out to the smallest detail. After the windows are planned and the background material is prepared, select the merchandise. (This could be done first and the idea developed around it, but this is usually more difficult.) Selecting merchandise is as much an art as displaying it. It should support the theme of the window, and make a beautiful picture as well. The window image should be immediately understandable. The easier it is to see and comprehend, the more impulse buying is encouraged. Simplicity — selling one idea at a time — is the key.

Select a complete costume for each unit with the theme in mind as well as an eye for fashion. For example, a ring, bracelet, pin or neckwear could be an ensemble. Color should also be considered. Display stones that are harmonious to each other in color and price. Costume jewelry and karat jewelry do not work well together. The image of fine jewelry is destroyed when placed alongside inexpensive pieces.

After you've made your selection, clean each piece thoroughly. Wipe off the watches and use jewelry-cleaning solution on stone rings and other items. Wear cosmetic gloves when handling cleaned jewelry so no fingerprints are left behind. When finished, take a few minutes to inspect and be certain everything is in proper order.

The show card is next to be prepared. It should contain five to seven words, using a lyrical theme that effectively identifies the product and store (see chapter on signage). Keep the message simple, avoid extreme statements and don't use pompous generalities or be deceptive. The product is of prime importance and the show card should reflect this. Also, carry the window's color theme into the card. A well-done show card should prod viewers into wanting more and better things — starting with your jewelry.

After preparations are finished for the new display, it's time to remove the old one. The first rule is: Never leave the window vacant of merchandise any longer than necessary during opening hours. Trim it as quickly as possible, with few trips to and from the window (hence, the benefits of those extensive preparations). This is also a time to be security conscious. Don't underestimate the person who is looking for an opportunity to steal a tray of jewelry. Keep merchandise out of easy reach, and lock the window if you're called away — even if only for a few minutes.

After the window is stripped, wash it inside and out. Check the light bulbs, replacing any that are defective. (Replacing all the bulbs at once is a good idea, since their efficiency diminishes with age.)

Vacuum the floor of the window and, if flooring is soiled or stained, change it. Nothing detracts more from merchandise than a dirty or faded floor, so keep that fabric fresh and clean.

Next, examine your commercial displayers. How many colors are being used? If more than two, the displayers might receive more attention than they deserve. Remember, it's jewelry being sold, not displayers. Are the displayers faded or worn? If so, it's time to dip into that merchandising budget and replace them.

Hold fast to this thought: The window is displaying the most precious commodity on the market, and it warrants only materials in fresh, clean condition.

In review, consider these steps when setting up your window:

- First, establish your target market.
- Next, formulate a theme.
- Shape the theme into a composition, and draw a layout.
- Fabricate background decorations and displayers.
- Select merchandise, and clean it.
- Prepare show cards and price markers.
- Remove the old display.
- Clean the window glass and display area.
- Check lighting.
- Clean displayers.
- Install the window setting.

After the display is complete, inspect it for any errors or maintenance needs. Continue this practice every day, scrutinizing all displays. Does the glass need cleaning again? Has any merchandise fallen over? Are the displayers and the display area clean? The job isn't finished until you can confidently say, "This is the best window I could create." You might not receive applause for a job well-done, but the rewards will come through an increase in sales.

Trimming the window takes on many aspects of market research. It encompasses knowing to whom a display is projected, what function the jewelry will perform, how consumers will use it and what they will pay for it. Keeping all this in mind, it's up to the display person to create a setting that will entice consumers to purchase the featured product. No part in the process should be omitted, and continued vigilance must be maintained to assure displays remain in good order. In short, trimming windows should be the responsibility of a person who has the hands of an artist, genius of a craftsman and mind of a salesperson.

Chapter Nine

special promotions

Special promotions are one of the most effective ways to increase sales. But putting them into action takes planning, a budget, knowing the lifestyle and values of customers and pinpointing the media that will best reach your customers.

Gail Rainwater, a sales consultant known for achieving astonishing gross sales with simple promotions, says the first step to a successful sales promotion is determining its purpose. Do you want to bring in new customers? Make customers aware of a new line of jewelry? Clear out old inventory?

Next, target your customers as to age, income and education. Then develop a promotion that offers merchandise in their price range and in a style that matches your market's sophistication. Regardless of income and education, your audience consists of individuals with special preferences who expect good service, value and selected pieces of jewelry.

Don't forget to invite the media. It offers them an opportunity for an article about area personalities and special business events. Let local stations broadcast live from your store. That always generates excitement.

Now begin to plan the event itself. First set a time and date. Be sure the date doesn't conflict with another special event in the area, and allow plenty of time for planning. Invitations have to be designed and printed. The color and shape should tie in with the promotion's theme. Keep in mind it takes time to address the invitations. They should be mailed out seven to 10 days before the day of the sale. A mailing list can be composed from receipts of customers who've purchased $200 or more from your store in a year's time.

Develop promotional plans on a frequency that best fits the area and establishment. Rainwater suggests that promotional sales be held monthly if they are kept simple. Also, involve your staff and the advertising media for suggestions of themes and ideas. Make it a fun event with all having a special part.

After the time and date are established, plan the advertising. The advertising campaign should be timed near the day of the event so that it also complements the invitations. Keep the ad clear, simple and in good taste, stressing the theme. Rainwater suggests you should remain open-minded to ideas offered by the media, since they are experienced in these endeavors.

A sample invitation might read:

> *You are invited to be our special guest*
> *at our*
> CHRISTMAS IN JULY TEA
> *(Date)*
> *(Time)*
> *We will have refreshments, special discounts*
> *Christmas lay-aways and great door prizes!*
> *We look forward to seeing you at this special event.*
> *(Store's Name)*
> *(Address and Phone Number)*

Attach a card to the invitation that says: "Bring this card to match the lucky numbers for $_____ of special prizes at (date and time). Add the store name at the bottom, along with a number assigned to that particular card.

Decorations and atmosphere should be tied to the theme. Napkins, decorations and employee attire are part of the party plan. Once again, keep it simple and in good taste. Refreshments might be made by store personnel to help defray costs, or hire a caterer. Cookies, finger food and candy might end up on the carpet, Rainwater cautions, so choose what cleans up easily. Fill punch cups only two-thirds full for less chance of spilling. If wine is served, make it white; red stains. And be sure to temper the amount of any alcoholic beverage served. Delegate a staff member to find extra help if necessary to greet guests and serve food. They often find reliable and less expensive helpers. And it's surprising how often a temporary helper can become one of your best customers after being exposed to and involved with lovely jewelry.

If special merchandise is connected with the sale, check with an insurance agent to see if additional coverage is needed. A security guard might be a good idea, since he can not only help direct large crowds, but also lends importance to the special pieces of merchandise on hand.

Remember to reward the help, maybe offering something special for the person who has the most sales, largest single sale, or brings in the most customers. This can be a big factor in the success of the promotion. Rainwater stresses that, along with planning promotional sales, there should be a working relationship in the organization that brings into play the cooperation and enthusiasm of the sales staff. Develop this special relationship by:

- Hiring people who get along well with others.
- Keeping your staff happy. Give praise when praise is due and try not to criticize employees when they are down. Instead, find them doing something right, and offer incentives.
- Make certain staff members are compatible, and encourage them all to follow the Golden Rule.
- Set aside a time each day for constructive thinking. This is very important. Establish five goals each day for self-improvement as well as improving the business. Each goes hand-in-hand.
- Keep good records of volume of stores and sales people. Have conferences on a regular basis to let sales staff know how they are progressing.
- Stress in each meeting that every sale that takes place aids not only the sales volume for the month, but for the year.
- Use each day as a learning experience.
- Set realistic goals and work out a plan to achieve them.

To keep promotion costs down, many sources may be used to gain momentum free of charge. For instance, you can often receive products and services in exchange for mentioning the contributor in your ads — such as a florist who has provided a dozen long-stem roses as a door prize, or a pizza parlor that might have provided bite-size pizza hors d'oeuvres as party refreshments. Again, use local businesses if possible.

During the party, keep track of who is attending, and circulate and see what merchandise is most admired. Note what customers are wearing, and what their lifestyle is like. Use what's learned on your next buying trip.

Rainwater offers the following suggestions for special promotion themes:

- Remount Promotion — Offer free cleaning of rings, check prongs and suggest new settings for old diamond rings. Show before-and-after designs, and photographs of new looks for diamonds. Bring the fashion of the season into the theme, and stress the importance of jewelry that complements it. Offer a larger discount for remounting to invitational customers only, less off to the general public. This emphasizes the importance of being your special customer.
- Color Consultant Promotion — Hire a color consultant on make-up and tie in the importance of colored stones in keeping with the individual's personal coloring. Have the sales representative from your colored stone supplier on hand to offer personalized advice and product information to customers. Any time personal attention is paid to a client, major sales are likely to follow.
- Fall Harvest Sale — Offer a "rainfall of savings" during autumn, giving away a beautiful "Fall Harvest" umbrella to your first 50 customers. The sale can focus on early holiday lay-aways and special gift purchases.
- Sporting Events — When baseball playoffs and football season roll around, it's a prime opportunity to feature sports watches and jewelry. Offer a chance to win a pair of tickets to the local college or professional game with every purchase. Feature photos of local athletes in windows, and decorate with the team colors.
- Business Women's Fashion Show — Coordinate this event with local department stores or boutiques to show off their professional women's fashion lines. Provide jewelry that complements these outfits — such as pearls for suits and tailored dresses, or a tasteful diamond pin to dress up a somber blouse. Also provide information on proper care of jewelry, and maybe offer a string of pearls as a doorprize. This coordinated fashion show offers a chance to share the costs of a promotion with local merchants in an effort that is certain to benefit all.
- For Men Only Evening — Contact men's service clubs in the area and invite them to an evening of special sales for holiday gifts. Men are nearly always happy to let someone help them with shopping. Hire a couple of attractive models to circulate, wearing jewelry gift items. All employees should be dressed in festive attire. Serve refreshments and make the occasion fun as well as helpful to the men who attend. Wrap the gifts with extra care, and distribute cards introducing a shopping service for company-related gifts, such as clocks, watches and jewelry for employees.
- Festival of Gems by Santa's Helpers — Have a trunk showing of jewelry for several of your best-selling suppliers. A good time to do this is the week after Thanksgiving, when everyone is in the holiday mood. You might even tie this in with a charity event, such as requesting all attendees bring a "Toys for Tots" gift. For each toy contributed, offer a 10-percent discount on a purchase

Photo: Richard Beauchamp

Cabochon Gems and Designs: designer — Judith Hooks, Display! by Judith Hooks, Milwaukee

C.D. Peacock, Chicago: designer — Joel Klaff, Chicago

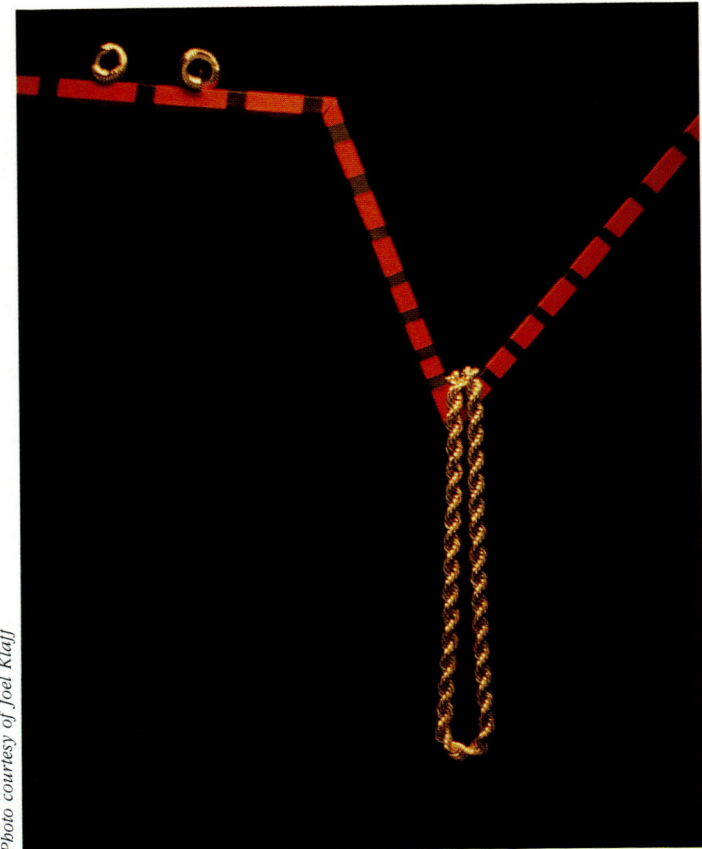

Photo courtesy of Joel Klaff

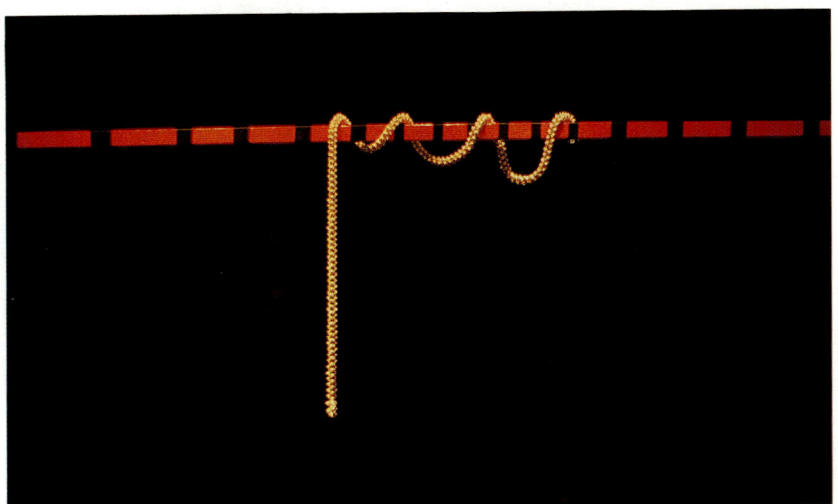

Lee Michaels Fine Jewelry, Lafayette, La.: designer — Jane Widas, Lafayette

Gucci, Atlanta: designer — Joel F. Griswold, Jr., Atlanta

Photo: David Powell Photographs, Atlanta

C.D. Peacock, Chicago: designer — Joel Klaff, Chicago

Photo courtesy of Joel Klaff

Tiffany & Co.: designer — Gene Moore, display director

Photo: © Jerry P. Melmed, New York City

Photo: © Jerry P. Melmed, New York City

Tiffany & Co.: designer — Gene Moore, display director

C.D. Peacock, Chicago:
designer — Joel Klaff,
Chicago

Photo courtesy of Joel Klaff

Photo courtesy of Joel Klaff

C.D. Peacock, Chicago: designer — Joel Klaff, Chicago

Frederic Goodman, Summit, N.J.: designer — International Design Group (USA) Inc., New York City

Photo: Scott Francis, New York City

Rogers & Hollands, Chicago: designer — DePalma Group Inc. (formerly Planning & Design Group, Inc.), Chicago

Photo: A.Y. Sato, Chicago

Tiffany & Co.: designer — Gene Moore, display director

Photo: © Jerry P. Melmed, New York City

C.D. Peacock, Chicago: designer — Joel Klaff, Chicago

Photo courtesy of Joel Klaff

Photo courtesy of Joel Klaff

C.D. Peacock, Chicago: designer — Joel Klaff, Chicago

Tiffany & Co., New York City: designer — Gene Moore, display director

Lee Michaels Fine Jewelry,
Lafayette, La.: designer
— Jane Widas, Lafayette

Lee Michaels Fine Jewelry,
Lafayette, La.: designer
— Jane Widas, Lafayette

of $50 to $200 and a chance to win a $100 gift certificate toward a diamond purchase in a lucky draw. Christmas decorations should already be in place, adding to your store's festive mood.

The possibilities for promotional themes are endless, limited only by your creativity. Once every member of the staff has been encouraged to participate in developing promotional ideas, a bountiful source will have been tapped. Collect all resources and suggestions, then refine them to fit your needs. Always consider costs and responses received from past promotions, then apply them to your new idea and give it a try.

Remember — it's not a sin to try and fail; it's only a sin to fail to try. Use the word "experiment," rather than "failure." If one promotion doesn't work to fullest expectations, profit from it. Call it an experiment, consider what went wrong and rectify that, then use this information when developing the next promotion. Learn to take basic foundations that build business and combine them with new ideas. Constantly promote growth, and climb till your goals are realized — then keep climbing.

Chapter Ten

Christmas is that time of year when all the world exudes love, so design your windows to promote jewelry as a fitting gift for this exciting holiday.

christmas

It's that time of year when all the world falls in love again, and every song seems to say "Merry Christmas." The symbol of love is jewelry, and Christmas is certainly jewelry time. Knowing the origin and lore behind many holiday symbols can help your windows relay the spirit of the season.

The Christmas tree was intially part of a pagan ritual. An evergreen would be brought indoors to sprout at the winter solstice (December 21-22), followed by a celebration of the sun's return along with longer days. The yule log is also a pagan symbol for winter solstice.

Paradise trees, laden with apples, were pagan rituals initially celebrated during this time, but adapted to the "praise of God" in 598 A.D. by England's Pope Gregory the Great. In the 15th century, the French began calling it the topiary tree.

Martin Luther of Germany is credited with introducing Christmas tree lights. He felt this represented Christ — the light of the world. We also have the Germans to thank for glass balls and fancy tinsel ornaments.

In Italy, in 1223, Saint Francis of Assisi was first to display a carved wooden Nativity. The ceppo, a wooden frame arranged in a pyramid with several tiers of shelves, held the Nativity scene. Its lower shelf was for the scene itself, while upper tiers held gifts for the Christ child. The ceppo was decorated with colored paper and gilded pine cones, with candles placed at the shelf corners. Its triangular shape symbolized fire, a pagan sign of the sun's return after winter solstice.

The most popular symbol of all, Santa Claus, was actually a 4th-century bishop, Saint Nicholas. Saint Nicholas was born in Asia Minor, but became the patron saint of countries from Russia to Holland and Lapland to Greece, due to his generosity.

America's Christmas is an adaptation of all these symbols and celebrations. It is interesting to note the Puritans forbade the observance of any Christmas celebration. But after the Revolutionary War, Christmas trees began to appear throughout the country, laden with decorations and sweets-filled cornucopias. Their introduction is credited to the Hessian mercenaries of the war. Virginia colonists introduced decorating with ivy, holly and rosemary. In 1909, in Pasadena, California, the practice of decorating an outdoor tree with electric lights began.

It's only natural that this most exciting holiday period of the year be reflected through carefully planned and executed display windows. Entertain the public with exquisite displays in windows that are both poignant and effectively utilize themes to nudge viewers toward buying jewelry.

The following holiday themes have proven successful:

- "Kindle Your Love With a Diamond"
- "Thrill With a Gift of Jewelry"
- "The Eloquence of Gems"
- "Diamonds: A Gift of Beauty"
- "Dazzle Him With a Gift of Jewelry"
- "Bejewel Her With Gems"
- "They're Gorgeous, They're Stunning, They're by (Your Name)"
- "One Gift That's Always Perfect — Jewelry"
- "Pearls — The Classic Gift"
- "Gold Is Forever"
- "Time by (Your Name) — The Perfect Gift"
- "The Discriminating Gift of Designer Jewelry"
- "Bestow a Gift of Love With Gems"
- "Santa, I Want a Diamond!"

Christmas displays might use traditional background materials, or draw upon the more unusual — maybe even a combination of both.

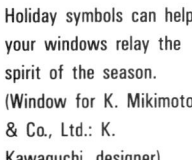

Holiday symbols can help your windows relay the spirit of the season. (Window for K. Mikimoto & Co., Ltd.: K. Kawaguchi, designer)

Words may suggest traditional background materials, or they may stimulate the imagination to use something different — the choice is yours. Just remember, you're not selling boxes of various shapes and colors made by suppliers. Beautifully crafted jewelry looks much more appealing on clean, unobtrusive displayers. Colors may be Christmas red and green, or a combination of your choice. Too many hues, however, vie with the jewelry for attention.

Planning, preparing and selecting the merchandise and theme for a sales-oriented Christmas takes time. Be sure to devote this attention to your working program. Correlate windows and advertising for maximum benefits.

Remove merchandise at night, but leave behind discreet signs stating the Christmas jewelry will return during shopping hours. Also, identify the sections of the windows that will house various merchandise. If there is heavy foot-traffic passing by at night, video sets might be put to good use to show the merchandise. Videos can feature advertised items, the month's birthstone or special gems.

Be sure the night windows, though bare, look clean and are in good repair. They may be empty, but they still show how much importance the establishment places on the value of the merchandise. Image prompts as many sales as knowledge of the gemstones.

Follow these simple rules and you can welcome with confidence that time of year when all the world exudes love. This confidence comes from knowing your windows are well-planned and well-executed to yield sales that will truly make yours a merry Christmas.

Chapter Eleven

displaying diamonds

The history of diamonds is as exciting as the scintillating fire from their 58 facets. From the power struggle to consolidate the diamond-rich African mines under one head, to controlling marketing of the bulk of the world's gem and industrial diamonds by the Central Selling Organization of London, to the purchase of parcels of uncut diamonds, there's no novel written that contains such intrigue.

History has been shaped by violence and tragedy as famous diamonds changed hands. Men have marched to battle with the assurance that diamonds' hardness would bring them courage and stamina. In the 15th century, they became royal symbols as gems for women who were members of the king's court. In 1866, when diamonds were discovered in Africa, world history was altered. Engagement diamonds, symbols of eternal love, are a distinctly American custom. As the Gay 90s swept the world, so did the brilliant-cut. It still holds all the world spellbound with its beauty.

Today, diamonds represent the greatest unit of sales in the jewelry industry. Their beauty makes them a much sought-after commodity. They are also sold as an investment and hedge against inflation. No longer thought of as only an engagement symbol, after-marriage diamond recipients have become the greatest source of large stone sales for the jewelry industry. This fact is key to determining the market age that displays should be directed toward.

Display only a few diamond pieces at a time to demonstrate their beauty and scarcity to best advantage. (Window for Zale Corp.: Art Smith and H. Neal Hay, designers)

What characteristics of diamonds should be taken into consideration when planning displays?

The diamond is a form of carbon whose hardness surpasses any other naturally occurring substance. It has a very high degree of transparency, and can be highly polished. Polishing diamonds enables them to reflect a great degree of light. This reflected light is known as a diamond's luster.

Diamonds refract, or bend, light and change its direction, which in turn causes interesting color effects. A diamond's extreme refraction can separate a ray of white light into the colors of a rainbow. This phenomenon is called dispersion. Dispersion is at its best in a diamond, as it produces a dazzling shower of separated color splashes, or fire.

Desirable colors in the fire of a diamond are blue, green, red and violet. These, then, become good choices for background display colors. They should be pigment-rich, but not vibrating. To enhance a diamond with a slight yellow body color, use yellow's complement — violet — or the split complement, blue-violet or red-violet. To emphasize a diamond's fire, display it on a red background. To show a diamond that is nearly free from body color, use its complement, black. Effectively displaying diamonds evidently takes a good understanding of color.

Lighting is another factor over which the displayer should exert strict control. Diamonds' high dispersion capabilities can be used to advantage in the display. The window's light should be pleasing in color — near white or daylight — and with a point source of incandescent.

A new low-voltage lamp on the market with a dichroic reflector is the MR16, which is perhaps the best source of light for selling diamonds. (For more information, see the chapter on lighting and Appendix.)

Fluorescent lamps will give an even, flat light with good color rendition. This is not a point source of light; therefore, it doesn't emphasize diamonds' scintillation. MR16 spots are excellent for highlighting diamond displays.

When considering lighting for the diamond area of your store, consider whether it will enhance the beauty of the diamond and at the same time be warm enough to flatter customers. (Incandescent is a good choice.) When selecting light sources for diamond grading areas, use cool lights or those dominated by blue (fluorescent).

Display only a few diamond pieces in each unit in order to demonstrate their beauty and rarity to the best advantage. Mass display implies a lack of scarcity and connotes inexpensiveness. This is not the setting for a diamond. Play up diamonds in the role for which they were intended, showing their brilliance, scintillation and fire.

What should your image be and who is the target audience? In 1949, when the slogan "A Diamond Is Forever" was created, it keyed the jewelry industry to a new approach in advertising. The slogan defined and pictured images the industry appealed to. One was directed to young people, encouraging the diamond engagement ring tradition. Another was to the middle-aged set, appealing to their pride of ownership and investment. The third was directed to senior citizens, who find diamonds appealing as family heirlooms. In this classic promotion, copy was low-key and illustrations were in fine artistic taste to match the elegance of diamonds. This campaign, by DeBeers Consolidated Mines, Ltd., through N.W. Ayer & Son, is still in progress to help support the sales efforts of jewelers.

A survey showed that 81 percent of all first-time brides receive diamond engagement rings. It also looked at jewelry purchases during Christmas for married women. Interestingly, when married women received diamond jewelry that cost $1,000 or more, their

Lighting is one factor that should be strictly controlled in diamond displays in order to benefit most from the gem's high dispersion capabilities. (Window for Cartier)

Photo: Malan Studio Inc., New York City

purchases seem to be spread throughout the year. The majority — 68 percent — of married women's purchases was made at some time other than Christmas. This indicates that diamonds should have a prominent place in all displays at all times.

Market research preceding an ad campaign should answer two questions to aid in developing display windows: the types and ages of the market, and the motive behind the purchase. Combine this information with the "Diamonds Are Forever" image, and you'll have infinite themes for diamond window displays.

Select diamond merchandise with complete ensembles in mind. Direct the lighting to most effectively show their dazzling fire, and present diamonds stressing these points: The display should be clean, fresh and in the proper color; allow the diamonds room to show off their exquisite qualities; and put them on the plateau of the most sought-after gem, but in a manner that suggests they are within the reach of the average person.

Diamonds account for the greatest amount of sales of all gems. This volume can increase even more if they are properly displayed.

Chapter Twelve

displaying watches

Watches constitute 50 percent of some jewelers' gross sales, and marketing experts predict they will continue as good unit and dollar gainers. It is evident, then, that watches are among the most important commodities on the jewelry market. Therefore, jewelers should understand how to display them.

Watch display relies on the principles of composition, color and good lighting. These fundamentals apply to any display in any window. Review them if necessary to refresh yourself on the essentials.

Objectives to keep in mind when displaying watches include:

- Show the watch face.
- Show the bracelet.
- Exhibit the physical features of the case.
- Expose special technical features (such as digital, solar, quartz, analog and underwater capabilities).

Present watches in units, just as with other types of jewelry, considering the display's composition, height, width and placement. Also, consider price, style and the functions the particular watch style performs. Think in terms of the watch's materials — white gold, yellow gold or leather straps. Each would be shown to the best advantage in a unit of its own kind.

Since watches are one of the most important commodities on the jewelry market, make certain the displays you create for them are attractive and effective. (Window for Cartier)

Photo: Malan Studio Inc., New York City

Present watches in units, considering the display's composition, height, width and placement. Other things to consider include price, style and the watches' functions.

Simple, inexpensive items can provide interesting backgrounds and relay the durability of the particular type of watch. (Window for F.D. Fogg & Co.: Lynn Daily, designer)

A point to stress: Take the watches out of their boxes. Each watch company box has its own color, shape and material. If left in their boxes, the window could become one big conglomeration.

Another point to keep in mind is that jewelers want their names to be projected and remembered by consumers. Therefore, use care that the watch companies' names receive less play than the merchant's. Watches do sell due to name brand, so use the neat metal company placards provided by the manufacturer with the unit displays.

Also, tell manufacturers' representatives what you liked or disliked about the commercial displays they sent. You are paying for them directly or indirectly, as they are figured into the cost of the product as advertising. These displays can be very helpful selling aids. Usually, manufacturers have national campaigns in progress that tie in with the window display sent you. Take advantage of this advertising, for here again you are paying for it.

Manufacturers' commercial displayers can be very helpful selling aids. Jewelers may often take advantage of national advertising campaigns that are tied in with the displayers.

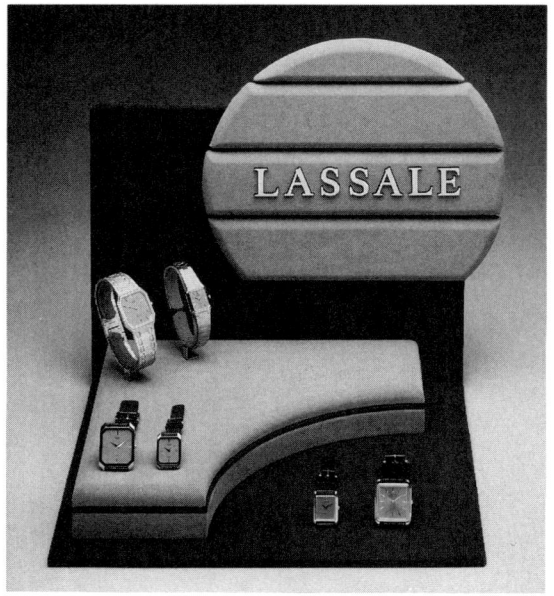

Consider these points for good, innovative watch displays:

- Watches placed horizontally on the window floor reflect light from the crystal, making them difficult to see.
- Tilt the watch so that customers may see the dial, hands, figures and case.
- Gold-bracelet watches are best shown with the bracelet in full view.
- Show pocket watches with the cases opened, or closed if the cases have special features.
- The slenderness of an extra-thin watch is effectively demonstrated by showing it from two angles — face-on and a side view.

Watches may be the whole theme for a window, or they may supplement other pieces of jewelry related in terms of appearance and price. The display could include dress watches, cuff links, tie tacks, money clips and 14K-gold belt buckles. Diving watches, knives, watch bands and rings may also be combined.

Watches may or may not be a big unit in your establishment, but in the overall jewelry market they rank second. So make an effort to display them in a creative manner. Promoting watches along with other jewelry increases the opportunity for additional sales, so try it.

Time is an important part of everyone's life, so let the windows sell timekeepers to all who pass by.

Chapter Thirteen

store planning

The 20 years between mid-1930 and mid-1950 were the Age of Recovery — recovery of capital lost in the Depression and recovery of management lost to World War II. By the mid-1950s, retailers were poised on the Age of Explosion — expanding their territories, exhausting their competition, updating techniques.

Retailers are now entering the Age of Knowledge, with more sophisticated know-how extended over a broadened spectrum of management, from financial to marketing to strategic planning. If muscle/size were all that mattered, as it once did, W.T. Grant would be alive today and Wal-Mart would be an obscure variety store in Arkansas.

The trend in the 1950s and 1960s to elaborate store decor is quietly dying. Expense may have been the initial trigger that's killing it off, but perceptive store designers now see the "ultimate look" as the merchandise itself. If a department looks complete before merchandise arrives, the design is a failure.

While old downtowns continue to disintegrate as retail centers, the new downtowns are doing very well indeed. What are these new downtowns? They are new office complexes rising in the old city retail centers. A good example is Wilshire Center in downtown Los Angeles, where The Broadway and other department stores have opened scaled-down versions geared to white-collar employees in surrounding office buildings. The office complex houses more than 30,000 workers, and shop hours are wisely patterned after office hours — as early as 8 a.m. openings, with no evening hours and most closed on weekends as well.

The next bulge in the U.S. population will be in the 25- to 44-year-old age bracket, according to the U.S. Census Bureau. This means a reciprocal decline in the ratio of school-aged children, but still it's altogether healthy for retailing. As K mart chief Bob Dewar sees it: "It is an age when discretionary income is expanding — when household formation takes place." These new demographics will also spur the doubling up of income producers and reduce the average number of children per household — spelling out higher spending potential.

This increased sales potential shouldn't solely benefit apparel — some sleeper departments, nestled in tiny spaces in the backwaters of major department stores, are realizing fantastic results. Some stores were lumping everything from jewelry to cosmetics to books and greeting cards into a single department. Under these circumstances, it wasn't always easy to identify profitable merchandise. Now, however, they're getting smart and splitting these groups into departments with their own national merchandise managers. New insights into the profit performance per-square-foot brought on this change. These small-wares lines, and that includes jewelry, occupy frugal space, yet return extremely high gross profits per dollar.

The trend to use elaborate store decor is dying, being replaced by designs that let the merchandise become the focal point. (Karten's Jewelers, by International Design Group (USA) Inc., New York City)

Photo: Scott Francis

A well-designed store should not only be visually pleasing, but comfortable for both customers and store personnel. (Rogers & Hollands, by DePalma Group, Inc. (formerly Planning & Design Group Inc.), Chicago)

Photo: A.Y. Sato, Chicago

Photo: A.Y. Sato, Chicago

Space allocation is key to planning any profitable store, and should be based on the items that stimulate the bulk of your income. (Rogers & Hollands, by DePalma Group, Inc. (formerly Planning & Design Group Inc.), Chicago)

Space allocation is key to planning any profitable store — whether it's a major department store or a small jewelry shop. Percentage-wise, where is the bulk of income — diamonds, colored stones, gold, watches, gifts, china? Who are your customers? Determine the market and project toward it. Remember, one cannot be everything to everybody. Gather information and decide what you wish to achieve within a given space. How many departments will the store have? How many offices, diamond rooms, how much space for employees?

Just as with merchandise presentation, store planning begins with editing the merchandise. What inventory will be stocked and how much space will it occupy? How will the staff dispense, sell and stock merchandise? What services will be offered, and what area will they occupy? Most important, how will customers' comfort, movement ease, and sense of well-being be addressed?

Store planning is committed to visually presenting and selling merchandise with customer and personnel comfort in mind. It should offer less design hype and more attention to merchandising and service requirements. Seek to use space productively and enhance the presentation of merchandise in order that it will be appealing. Design space for the customer — open space. Open space makes the interior more attractive and the staff's efforts more productive.

Start designing the store by listing merchandise as to percentage of income. Merchandise that produces a large volume of sales is ordinarily given the most valuable store area. A good planning outline would include:

1. Interior Design — Aesthetics and Comfort
   A. Space planning
   B. Lighting
   C. Color
   D. Acoustics
   E. Graphics, signage
   F. Comfort (heating, air conditioning)

2. Facilities Planning
   A. Work flow — movement of people
   B. Number of workers
   C. Relationship of workers to organization and to each other
   D. Space standards — space per person
   E. Furniture and equipment — shop and selling

3. People
   A. Behavioral aspects of design
   B. Individual work stations
   C. Type of furniture

D. Diamond room and office — size and location

4. Organizational Structure
   A. Departmental duties
   B. Lines of frequent communication
   C. Work functions
   D. Specific tasks performed
   E. Privacy requirements
   F. Special equipment requirements
   G. Individual work-station needs

5. Communication
   A. Personnel relationships
   B. Priority relevant to the work flow
   C. Need for shared facilities
   D. Paper flow for sales information — present and future

6. Contents
   A. Space, elevations, electrical, water, gas, sewer, air conditioning, sprinklers
   B. Display cases
   C. Interior decor
   D. Specifications

7. Regulations
   A. Compliance with local, state and federal regulations with regard to environment, energy, OSHA, etc.

This outline pinpoints considerations that must be satisfied. Each category is complete in itself, but interrelated to the whole planning process. Planning the interior for aesthetics and comfort requires someone with architectural and/or construction knowledge, someone who knows the limits of materials, is familiar with local building codes, and has an appreciation for jewelry. The designer compiles data on merchandise space requirements and fashions a traffic pattern that graciously leads customers through the store and allows personnel adequate workspace — comparable to weaving fibers into a pattern. Remember that all planning and designing must meet local and federal government requirements in order to obtain a construction permit.

A word of advice to jewelers: Have a contract stating all work to be done and what the contractor will do for a given sum. A contract makes for a good working relationship between client and contractor. If possible, have a time clause within the contract stating how long it will take to complete the project and any penalties the contractor will pay if it is not done on time. Get receipts for payments for labor and materials. Include everything in the plans for a

Open space makes a jewelry store's interior more attractive and the staff's efforts more productive.

turn-key project. Any changes or deviations result in extra charges. For additional protection, insurance can be purchased. See your agent for more details.

The store should be as spacious as possible, with attention paid to finishing details. The impact of color and lighting that is used to direct or pull people to various areas warrants much thought. Lighting should be bright to give a feeling of cheerfulness, and to help evaluate gems in a true rendition of their color. Remember that the owners and staff must function every day in the environment, so it should be pleasing to all. Walls should be light, with intense colors saved for accents in wall displays and artwork. Jewelry stores are generally small and dark colors tend to reduce an area, which is another reason for using light, cheerful colors.

Provide a sense of order so that the planning is not merely a design, but part of the function of a store. Offer customers a place to sit down in comfortable chairs for major sales. Help them shop without a lot of hassles, for they often have little time to waste.

Offer ample space for interior displays, where suggestions for wearing the jewelry and information about gems and designs can be provided. The wall area is for displaying merchandise, not stocking. Back-up stock should be kept out of sight in accessible drawers and cupboards.

Space planning must be organized around security, especially in a jewelry store, so all drawers, cupboards and display cases should be kept locked. Insurance companies often have requirements that must be met. Be sure they are known by the designer, and not side-stepped (see chapter on security).

Research your store plan thoroughly, and listen with an open mind as to functions that are part of a jewelry store, then offer space to accommodate them. Design a store that offers customers a cheerful, well-lighted atmosphere to shop in. And remember — the store isn't intended as a monument to the designer or architect, but to the gracious sale of jewelry.

Color and lighting can be used to direct or pull customers to various areas of the store. (Bermuda, by MariAnn Coutchie, Diversified Design, Woodland Hills, Calif.)

Photo: Scott Francis

An attractive store can increase the worth of the jewelry, making it look more valuable due to its surroundings. (Topaz, by International Design Group (USA) Inc., New York City)

Chapter Fourteen

security tips

Improving security to reduce insurance costs is one of the top concerns of every jeweler. Jewelers Mutual Insurance Co. has the following suggestions:

- The more merchandise kept in the safe, the lower the premium will be. Reduce show window coverage. Keep a minimum of inventory on the premises, and use a bank vault for excess merchandise or special merchandise. UL-listed alarms and hold-up buttons reduce premium rates, as does good experience. UL-listed alarm systems and safes with time locks and/or relock devices also lower insurance costs, while non-UL listed ones do not. Burglars can break into the store from an adjacent store that might not be equipped with an alarm. Keep your safes away from common walls, because burglars can attack the safe without entering the store.
- A closed-circuit television with videotape recorder is a good deterrent to daytime losses. It can also show a loss occurred that might otherwise go unnoticed. It's more difficult for dishonest employees to conceal a crime when they're virtually "on camera."

- Unless the vault is built to UL specifications, Jewelers Mutual prefers using more than one safe, since once in a vault burglars have access to all the contents. Multiple safes generally slow a burglar down and provide better protection against total loss. (The vault door should be of an equal burglary rating as its other five sides. All standing safes should be rated Tr T1 30x6.)
- Keep most merchandise in the safe when the store is closed. As a general rule, items that cost $100 or more wholesale should be locked in the safe at night. Burglar alarms are not effective loss-prevention tools for those three-minute "smash, grab and run" night-time losses, so remove merchandise from windows at night and lock it up.
- Do not open or close a store alone. This is the prime time for a robber to hit a store. Also, merchandise is concentrated in the safe or vault at this time, making large losses possible. In addition, the threat of physical injury is higher for one person.
- Sneak-thief losses are often less than the insurance deductible, so they often come straight from the jeweler's pocket. But these types of losses are very preventable, just by keeping showcases locked and showing only one item at a time. The reduction in losses will also keep insurance premiums down, as jewelers get up to a 50-percent credit on the crime portion of an insurance premium when losses paid do not exceed 50 percent of the premium paid over a five-year period.
- Enclosed malls tend to be more prone to daytime theft and less prone to burglary attacks on safes. Burglars do, however, find it easy to hide in a mall and break through roll-down gates after hours. Put all high-priced merchandise in a safe, and make certain the gate enclosing the store is of a high-grade material that resists cutting and/or bending. Aluminum gates are not recommended for this reason.
- Mall traffic does not deter daytime thefts or armed robberies. Thieves have an ability to disappear into the crowd and escape unnoticed. Guards employed by malls, either at night or during the day, have not proven to be effective loss deterrents either. Being located farther away from the entry door of the mall can be a plus, since thieves would have to run farther to escape the mall.
- Strip malls and other locations where stores share a common wall tend to be targets for armed robbery and burglary. Keep more than one person on the premises at all times. This is particularly important because other occupants of the mall cannot observe your store's interior.
- As much as 50 percent of an insurance premium can be generated by the fire rate. Fire rates are based on the quality of the local fire department, and the construction and contents of the building. If moving your business, find out the fire rates of various locations under consideration. Contact an insurance agent and re-

quest additional information that will help keep insurance rates down as much as possible in constructing your new store, as well as for planning its security.

Chapter Fifteen

photographing your window

Just as with display, photographing a window takes into consideration the principles of composition, light and color. The window can be photographed at an angle or straight on. Shadows, flat lighting or spotlighting a portion of the window can add drama. The picture can be done in either color or black and white — all these options are up to the photographer. Know what is to be captured on film, and this will give the key to the message of the picture. Like windows, pictures with themes tell better stories.

For best results, hire a professional photographer. If you can't afford one, maybe a friend who is a devoted amateur photographer could be persuaded to shoot the windows. If you opt to take the photograph yourself, the following guidelines should help obtain the best possible results.

Just as with display, photographing a window takes into consideration the principles of composition, light and color. (Window for Underwood's Fine Jewelers)

First, decide the objective of the photo. Is it a record to remember a theme? How well the window sold merchandise? What colors were used? How the window was composed? Or what was the effect of the lighting? Maybe it's to be used for an advertisement or contest. Possibly, you want to submit it with a news release. (If this is the case, a black-and-white photo should suffice. Most newspapers want a glossy 8x10 print. Magazines, however, vary in their requirements. It's best to check with the publication beforehand.)

In taking the photo, use the largest format camera available. The bigger the negative, the better the print it produces. Also, use a wide-angle lens if available. A wide-angle not only lets you get closer to the window to take your picture, but reduces reflections as well.

Next, choose the film type. T-Max (by Eastman) is a good, fine grain black-and-white film, available in 35mm or 4x5 sizes. For color, Fujichrome 400 offers good quality slides, while Fujicolor 400 results in exceptional prints. These films are some of the best on the market today. With each roll of film, an instruction sheet states its speed, called the ASA (how fast the film is or how sensitive it is to light). ASA stands for American Standards Association, which sets the standards for measuring film speed and specifying colors, etc. The ASA number on the camera must be set to match that of the film being used.

The camera's "F-stop" controls the diaphragm, or lens opening. This serves a double function — it varies the amount of light that reaches the film, and controls the depth of field. Depth of field determines the depth of the picture that is in focus. For instance, if a

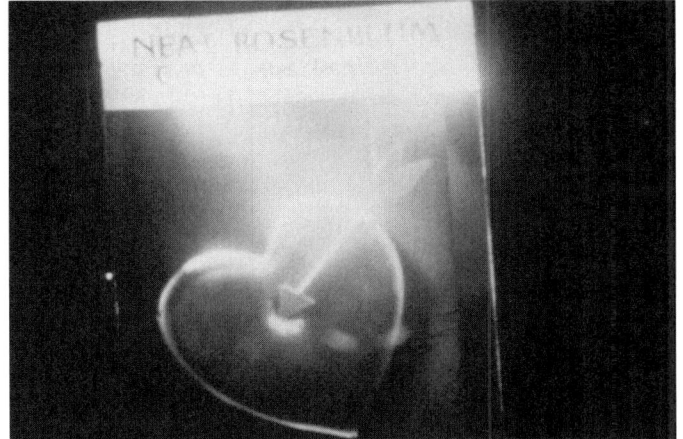

Taking photographs at night and using a dark cloth to block unwanted images can help prevent distracting reflections in your pictures.

Using a flash will cause a bright splash of light in photographs, as the flash reflects off the window glass.

wide opening of the lens, such as F2, is used, only a shallow portion of the picture will be in focus. (This is good for taking closeups, when the main emphasis is on the subject in the foreground, such as in an outdoors portrait.) But if the lens is "stopped down" to F22, most of the picture will be in focus — such as in a landscape scene. Generally, use greater depth of field when photographing a window. When choosing the combination of shutter speed and exposure time, use a large F-stop number and a longer exposure time. (F11 is a good, all-purpose setting.)

Setting the camera on a tripod helps prevent blurred pictures, since it's hard to hold the camera steady when releasing the shutter, especially when using shutter speeds below 60. Now look into the viewfinder and compose the picture. Be aware of all you see through the viewfinder. Is only the desired image visible? If not, move the camera to the correct angle and image.

Decide which part of the window will be the center of interest and take a reading of this area with a light meter. (Most cameras today have built-in light meters. However, hand-held versions are also available.) To make certain you are getting the right exposure, it's wise to "bracket" exposures, i.e., take three different photographs at three different F-stop settings, opening up one F-stop each time. Don't be cheap with film — getting a good picture is the prime objective here.

Windows photograph better at night, because there is less reflection on the glass then. To cut reflections to a minimum, cover the tripod legs with a black cloth secured with a couple of clothespins. Then hold an opaque cloth (a car blanket is the perfect size) up high enough behind the camera to eliminate the glow of street lights and signs. Look into the viewfinder and check for reflections. Move the position of the blanket until reflections are at a minimum. Then capture the image with a firm, gentle press of the shutter release.

Remember: Do not use a flash. It will reflect off the glass and cause a bright splash of light in each picture.

Be cautious of composition when photographing a window, especially if the photo will be submitted for publication in a magazine or newspaper. If an object is directly behind another piece of jewelry, even if the height is different, it will capture or compress them into one plane. The three-dimensional image of the window becomes one-dimensional on a photograph. Trim the windows rather light, or the picture will be too "busy" to be acceptable for publication.

For contest photographs, the theme (or background) should be very evident and well-defined in shape and light. The merchandise should be placed in a very definite composition, with no piece of jewelry in front of another, and its focal point should be in sharp focus and well-lit. The window should be only lightly trimmed, with a clear, well-composed message.

To photograph a window for information purposes only, shoot it as it appears. Have a tape measure handy for measuring how far away from the window your camera is placed — 5 feet seems to present the image at its best. (Always carry a 5-foot string in your camera bag as a quick reference.)

When using a Polaroid camera (not good for reproducing in publications), follow specific camera guidelines to capture a pleasing, well-focused picture. The closest distance a Polaroid can focus is 3½ feet; for focusing less than that distance, use a portrait or close-up kit.

Cameras may present variable methods of capturing the picture, but the end result should be the same: a picture that tells a message of beauty, information or method. It should be in sharp focus, with lighting beamed at the focal point and with a pleasing composition. Practice photographing windows, noting all film exposures and camera settings. This will reduce the amount of time and effort to produce good pictures in the future.

glossary

Analogous colors Colors that share a common hue (such as yellow and orange), with both being either warm or cool. Analogous colors lie next to or near each other on the color wheel.

Analogous with a complementary accent A color scheme consisting of two analogous colors and a complementary color accent.

Asymmetrical composition A composition arranged in a three-part grouping, consisting of a focal, intermediate and subordinate point, forming a visual triangle. Asymmetrical compositions relate a sense of excitement and innovation.

Color rendition The ability of a light source to adequately present the true colors of an object or environment.

Color wheel The hues present in a color spectrum, arranged in a circle in order of their appearance within the spectrum.

Composition The manner in which merchandise is arranged in a window, in an artistic combination.

Complementary colors Two colors that create white light when passed together through a glass prism. These contrasting hues lie directly opposite each other on the color wheel.

Cool colors The colors green, blue, violet or their variations, that appear as the sun goes below the horizon or in shaded areas. Cool colors are considered sedate.

Cool light Light with a bluish cast that is similar to natural daylight, such as that produced by fluorescent lamps.

Display The art of presenting merchandise in a manner that not only is attractive and tells a story, but entices sales.

Focal point The position slightly above center of a composition, to the left or right, that first attracts attention and is the starting point of the eye pattern. Visually, this is the most important point in a composition and should dominate in height and width placement.

Grumbacher color computer A color wheel that serves as a standard guide in color composition.

Height point The tallest visual line along which featured merchandise in a window display should be placed. The height point should be located slightly above the line that visually bisects the window's height.

Intermediate color A color formed by combining a primary and a secondary color.

Intermediate point The second-most important position in a composition, located to the right or left of the focal point at about one-third its height.

Monotone settings Settings in which one color is used.

Monochromatic scheme A setting consisting of a single hue in a variety of intensities and values, such as red, hot pink and light pink.

Near-complementary color scheme A color scheme consisting of colors that are not true complements, but are positioned near the true complement on the color wheel.

Presentation displayer A form on which jewelry is placed and held in position for viewing.

Primary colors The three pure colors — red, yellow and blue — which cannot be formed by mixing other colors, but from which are all other colors are composed.

Point The standard unit of measurement used by printers to determine typeface sizes. One point equals approximately 1/72 inch.

Secondary color A color formed by mixing two primaries.

Shade The resulting hue made by adding to a color either gray or its complement.

Show card A point-of-purchase advertising sign designed to quickly attract attention. (Also called "reader.")

Split complement Colors that lie near each other on the color wheel, separated by their true complement.

Subordinate point The point opposite the intermediate point in a composition, at about two-thirds its height.

Symmetrical composition Compositions with balanced proportions of size, shape and relative positioning of parts on opposite sides. Symmetrical compositions relate a sense of dignity.

Tint The resulting hue when white is added to a color.

Tone The resulting hue when black is added to a color.

Triadic harmony A color scheme consisting of two complements plus a third accent color.

Visual merchandiser A professional trained in the art of display.

Warm colors The colors red, orange, yellow and their variations, that are associated with the sun. Warm colors are considered active and full of vitality.

Warm light Light with an orange or yellowish cast, such as that produced by a flame source or incandescent lamp.

appendix: materials sourcelist

manufacturers' index

Fixtures & Components

California
B&N Industries
C&H Store Equip. Co.
A. Geo. Diack, Inc.
Diversified Design, MariAnn Coutchie
Foga Systems, Inc.
Magic Glass
Peter Pepper Products
Reeve Store Equip. Co.

Canada
Allied Store Equip. Ltd.
Dalco Commercial Concepts
Otema Store Fixtures, Ltd.

Georgia
Spacewall Int'l.

Illinois
Merchandising Equip. Group (MEG)
Opto Int'l.
Reflector Hardware Corp.
Roberts Colonial House Inc.

Kentucky
The Butler Group

Louisiana
J. Haws & Assoc.

Maine
Joslin Displays Inc.

Maryland
Hisson's Enterprises Inc.

Michigan
Amstore Corp.
Panel Processing, Inc.

Minnesota
Carlson Store Fixtures
Perma Groove Inc.
Stylmark Inc.

Missouri
  Jahabow Industries, Inc.
  The Nu-Era Group
  Spartan Showcase Inc.

Nebraska
  Omaha Fixtures Mfg.

New Jersey
  All Industries
  Astra Products, Inc.
  Pam Int'l. Co.
  Sama Plastics Corp.
  Store Best Corp.

New Mexico
  Customcraft Fixtures Inc.

New York
  Barrett Hill
  George Dell
  Econoco Corp.
  Greenwich Fixture Co.
  Kason Industries Inc.
  The Shepherd Corp.

Ohio
  ATM Enclosures Inc.
  American Showcase Co.
  Baker Store Equipment Co.
  Columbus Show Case Co.
  Dayton Showcase Co.
  The Marlite Organization
  Worthington Plastics & Supply Co.

Pennsylvania
  Custom Concepts, Inc.
  Dlubak Corp.
  Modern Plastics Corp.
  Shore Panel Co., Inc.

Vermont
  Clear Solutions, Inc.

Virginia
  Acme Fixtures Co.
  Display Systems, Inc.

Showcase Hardware & Locks

California
  EB Bradley Co.
  A. Geo. Diack
  Reeve Store Equip. Co.

Illinois
  Capitol Hardware Mfg. Co., Inc.

Jewelry Displayers

Arizona
  Arizona Case Inc.

California
  Los Angeles Window Display Co.
  Princess Tanya Inc.

Florida
  Bufkor Inc.
  Graves Co.

Kansas
  File-A-Gem

New Jersey
  The Alsten Co.

New York
  Edwin Freed Inc.
  Rocket Jewelry Box

Rhode Island
  Presentation Box
  (Div. of Int'l. Pkg. Corp.)

Texas
  Chippenhook Ltd.

Fabric

California
  Los Angeles Window Display Co.

Illinois
  Coral of Chicago

New York
  Dazian Fabrics

Rhode Island
  Presentation Box
  (Div. of Int'l. Pkg. Corp.)

Signage & Graphics

California
  Color 2000, Inc.
  Custom Color Lab
  DSA/Phototech
  Van Pelt Photographer

Florida
  Gamma Technologies, Inc.
  Scott Plastics Co.

Georgia
  Lettersigns Inc.

Kentucky
  Ad-Mart Inc.

Maine
  Display Concepts, Inc.

Michigan
  Meteor Photo Co.

Minnesota
  Clearr Corp.

New Jersey
  Letter Craft Inc.

New York
  Big Apple Signs
  Electra Letters
  Polyplastic Forms, Inc.

Ohio
  Trans Lights, Inc.

Oklahoma
  Central Sales Promotions, Inc.

Pennsylvania
  Filmet Color Labs

Texas
  Meisel Commercial Photographic

Lighting

California
  Capri Lighting
  Danalite
  Inlite Corp.

Florida
  Precision Industries

Georgia
  Lithonia Lighting

Illinois
  Alkco Lighting Co.
  ESV Inc.

Massachusetts
  GTE Sylvania

New Jersey
  Amerlux
  Econo-lite Products Inc.
  Lightolier, Inc.
  North American Philips Lighting Corp.

New York
  Farralane Ent., Inc.
  Lazin Lighting, Inc.
  Lighting Services Inc.
  Roxter Mfg. Corp.
  Staff Lighting Corp.
  Times Square Lighting
  VL Service Lighting

Ohio
  General Electric Lighting
  Venture Lighting, Int'l.

Oregon
  Grand & Benedicts

Washington
  Columbia Lighting Co.

Materials

Florida
  Interlam

Illinois
  Elgin Precision Glass

Maryland
  Nevamar Corp.

Michigan
  Ram Products

Minnesota
  Winona Industries

New Jersey
  Formica Corp.

North Carolina
  Advanced Technology, Inc.

Ohio
  Libby Owens Ford Co.

Oklahoma
  Cameron Glass, Inc.

Pennsylvania
  Consolidated Glass Corp.
  Laminated Glass Corp.
  PPG Industries, Inc.

Texas
Wilsonart

Virginia
Harwood Protection Industries Inc.

Miscellaneous

Alabama
Rainwater Diamond & Gold Warehouse

California
Cactus Mat Mfg. Co.
Charlotte Co.

Canada
Otema Store Fixtures Ltd.

Michigan
Worden Co.

New York
George Dell

The following is a list of manufacturers and distributors of products pertaining to jewelry display and store design. For a more extensive listing, see *VM + SD* magazine's annual *Buyers' Guide*.

Fixtures & Components

ATM Enclosures Inc.
29075 Solon Rd.
Cleveland, OH 44139
216-248-9000
800-527-7898
Product: Showcases

Acme Fixture Co.
P.O. Box 26372
Richmond, VA 23260
804-232-4578
Products: Architectural elements; fixtures & components

All Industries
1591 Rt. 37 W., Bldg. G-2
Toms River, NJ 08753
201-244-8600
Product: Countertop fixtures

Allied Store Equipment Ltd.
625 Powell St.
Vancouver, BC V6A 3P9
CANADA
604-253-4511
800-663-4870 (In- and Out-of-state)
Products: Fixtures & components

American Showcase Co.
Ste. #207F
77 E. Wilson Bridge Rd.
Worthington, OH 43085
614-848-4406
Product: Showcases

Amstore Corp.
P.O. Box 6
716 Nims St.
Muskegon, MI 49443
616-722-6681
800-221-0287 (Out-of-state)
Product: Showcases

Astra Products, Inc.
238 Lindbergh Pl.
Paterson, NJ 07503-2817
201-278-7800
Product: Countertop fixtures

B & N Industries, Inc.
1300 Industrial Way, Unit #21
San Carlos, CA 94070
415-593-4127
800-424-4446 (In-state)
Product: Showcases

Baker Store Equipment Co.
18976 Cranwood Pkwy.
Cleveland, OH 44128
216-475-5900
Products: Fixtures & components

Barrett Hill Inc.
133 W. 25th St.
New York, NY 10001
212-242-4745
Products: Showcases & countertop fixtures

The Butler Group
P.O. Box 966
1901 S. Seventh St.
Louisville, KY 40201
502-636-3461
800-626-1574 (Out-of-state)
Product: Showcases

C & H Store Equipment Co.
1406 S. Los Angeles St.
Los Angeles, CA 90015
213-748-7165
800-648-4979 (In-state)
Product: Showcases

Carlson Store Fixtures
26 N. Fifth St.
Minneapolis, MN 55403
612-375-1606
800-328-8043 (Out-of-state)
Products: Showcases & countertop fixtures

Clear Solutions, Inc.
P.O. Box 2460
W. Brattleboro, VT 05301
802-257-7052
800-257-4550 (Out-of-state)
Product: Countertop fixtures

Columbus Show Case Co.
850 W. Fifth Ave.
Columbus, OH 43212
614-299-3161
800-848-3573 (Out-of-state)
Product: Showcases

Continental Wood Products, Inc.
7990 W. 25th Ave.
Hialeah, FL 33016
305-558-6442
Products: Architectural elements; fixtures & components

Counterbalance
12303 Montague St.
Pacoima, CA 91331
213-875-0307
Product: Countertop fixtures

Crown Metal Mfg. Co.
5925 S. Lowe Ave.
Chicago, IL 60621
312-873-3833
Product: Countertop fixtures

Crown Store Equipment Co.
P.O. Box 400
1302 Kittle Rd.
Holland, OH 43528
419-865-1394
Product: Showcases

Custom Concepts, Inc.
Oak Rd.
Gibsonia, PA 15044
412-265-3900
Products: Jewelry pads, build-ups and case liners

Customcraft Fixtures, Inc.
4914 Pan American Fwy.
Albuquerque NM 87109
505-881-9200
Products: Architectural elements; fixtures & components; lighting

Dalco Commercial Concepts
1125 Tupper St.
Hawkesbury ON K6A 3E1
CANADA
613-632-0973
Product: Showcases

Dayton Showcase Co.
2601 W. Dorothy Ln.
Dayton, OH 45439
513-294-0321
Product: Showcases

George Dell, Inc.
133 W. 25th St.
New York, NY 10001
212-206-8460
Product: Countertop fixtures

A. Geo. Diack, Inc.
1250 Johnson Dr.
Industry, CA 91745
818-961-2491
Product: Showcases

Display Systems, Inc.
P.O. Box 1031
Chilhowie, VA 24319
703-646-8779
800-648-8700 (Out-of-state)
Product: Slatwall

**Diversified Design,
MariAnn Coutchie**
22018 Ybarra Rd.
Woodland Hills, CA 91364
818-347-8922
Products: Architectural elements; space planning & interior design; fixtures; lighting

Dlubak Corp.
904 Freeport Rd.
Freeport, PA 16229
412-295-5167
800-336-0562 (Out-of-state)
Product: Showcases

Econoco Corp.
300 Karin Ln.
Hicksville, NY 11801
516-935-7700
800-645-7032 (Out-of-state)
Product: Countertop fixtures

Foga Systems, Inc.
31260 Cedarvalley Dr.
Westlake Village, CA 91362
818-706-3117
Product: Showcases

Greenwich Fixture Co., Inc.
45 Dobbin St.
Brooklyn, NY 11222
718-387-8425
Product: Showcases

J. Haws & Assoc.
8528 Line Ave.
Shreveport, LA 71106
318-861-3513 (In-state, call collect);
800-426-5181 (Out-of-state)
Product: Jewelry pads, build-ups and case liners; lighting; fabric; signage

Hisson's Enterprises, Inc.
8500 Parkdale Ave.
Baltimore, MD 21211
301-669-2244
Products: Architectural elements; fixtures & components

Jahabow Industries, Inc.
P.O. Box 507
Owensville Industrial Pk.
Owensville, MO 65066
314-437-4151
Product: Showcases

Joslin Displays Inc.
327 Mystic Ave.
Medford, MA 02155
617-396-4700; 800-325-4150 (In-state);
800-325-1030 (Out-of-state)
Products: Showcases & countertop fixtures

Kason Industries, Inc.
Colesville Rd.
Binghamton, NY 13902-1075
607-724-7225
Products: Showcases & countertop fixtures

Norman Lapin Display Fixtures
12 Charles St.
P.O. Box 301
Needham, MA 02194
617-444-0144
Products: Showcases & countertop fixtures

Magic Glass Co.
2345 Harrison St.
San Francisco, CA 94110
415-648-3000
Product: Showcases

**The Marlite Organization
Sub. USG Interiors, Inc.**
202 Harger St.
Dover, OH 44622
800-321-4404 (Out-of-state)
Product: Slatwall

Merchandising Equipment Group (MEG)
3025 W. Salt Creek Ln.
Arlington Heights, IL 60005
312-398-3338
800-323-7710
Products: Showcases & slatwall

Modern Plastics Corp.
152 Horton St.
Wilkes-Barre, PA 18702
717-822-1124
Product: Countertop fixtures

The Nu-Era Group
727 N. 11th St.
St. Louis, MO 63101
314-231-3662; 800-392-3661 (In-state);
800-325-7003 (Out-of-state)
Products: Showcases & countertop fixtures

Omaha Fixture Mfg.
10320 'J' St.
Omaha, NE 68127
402-592-3720
800-637-2257 (Out-of-state)
Product: Countertop fixtures

Opto International
65 E. Palatine Rd., Ste. 109
Prospect Heights, IL 60070
312-541-8462
Product: Showcases

Otema Store Fixtures Ltd.
101 Dan Park Rd.
Markham, ON L3R 1C2
CANADA
416-475-1066
Product: Showcases

Pam International Co., Inc.
P.O. Box 2043
S. Hackensack, NJ 07606
201-440-2100
800-524-1294 (Out-of-state)
Product: Showcases

Panel Processing Inc.
120 N. Industrial Ave.
Alpena, MI 49707
517-356-9007
800-433-7142 (Out-of-state)
Product: Slatwall

Peter Pepper Products
17929 S. Susana Rd.
Compton, CA 90224
213-979-0815
Products: Showcases & countertop fixtures

Perma Groove Inc.
P.O. Box 1016
Lakeville, MN 55044
612-469-4961
Product: Slatwall

Reeve Store Equipment Co.
9131 E. Bermudez St.
Pico Rivera, CA 90660
213-949-2535
Products: Showcases & countertop fixtures

Reflector Hardware Corp.
1400 N. 25th Ave.
Melrose Park, IL 60160
312-345-2500
Product: Showcases

Roberts Colonial House Inc.
570 W. 167th St.
S. Holland, IL 60473
312-331-6233
Product: Slatwall

Sama Plastics Corp.
800 Eastern Way
Carlstadt, NJ 07072
201-896-8080
Product: Countertop fixtures

The Shepherd Corp.
270 Middle Rd.
Henrietta, NY 14467
716-334-0022
800-289-5000
Products: Showcases & slatwall

Shore Panel Co. Inc.
P.O. Box 6859
2905 N. 16th St.
Philadelphia, PA 19132
215-229-9400
800-523-0143 (Out-of-state)
Product: Slatwall

Spacewall International
P.O. Box 482
Stone Mountain, GA 30086
404-294-9564
800-241-6637 (Out-of-state)
Product: Slatwall

Spartan Showcase Inc.
P.O. Box 470
Union, MO 63084
314-583-4050
800-325-0775 (Out-of-state)
Products: Jewelry pads, build-ups and case liners; lighting

Store Best Corp.
38-56 Long Ave.
Hillside, NJ 07205
201-289-1400
Products: Fixtures & components

Stylmark, Inc.
P.O. Box 32008
Minneapolis MN 55432
612-574-7474
800-328-2495 (Out-of-state)
Product: Showcases

Worthington Plastics & Supply Co.
P.O. Box 26627
Columbus, OH 43226
614-846-7890
800-999-7890
Products: Showcases & countertop fixtures

Showcase Hardware & Locks

A. Geo. Diack
1250 Johnson Dr.
Industry, CA 91745
818-961-2491
Products: Showcase locks; metal extrusions; sliding door track; frames

EB Bradley Co.
5080 S. Alameda St.
Los Angeles, CA 90058
213-749-3127
800-423-9190 (In-state)
Products: Specialty hardware; shelf brackets; cabinet pulls; sliding door locks

Capitol Hardware Manufacturing Co., Inc.
400 N. Leavitt St.
Chicago, IL 60612
312-666-5182
Products: Showcase locks & hardware

Reeve Store Equipment Co.
9131 E. Bermudez St.
Pico Rivera, CA 90660
213-949-2535
Product: Shelf brackets

Jewelry Displayers

The Alsten Company
Harbor Side Financial Center
300 Plaza 3
Jersey City, NJ 07311-3898
201-432-9550
800-526-3035 (Out-of-state)
Products: Jewelry displayers; risers; boxes

Arizona Case Inc.
5755 N. 51st Ave., #3
Glendale, AZ 85301
602-931-3691
800-528-0195 (Out-of-state)
Products: Gem holders; jewelry displayers; stone paper boxes; zip-lock bags

Bufkor, Inc.
2600 118th Ave.
St. Petersburg, FL 33716
813-579-9991
Products: Jewelry displayers; risers

Chippenhook Ltd.
3105 Justin Rd.
Lewisville, TX 75028
214-539-1672
800-527-5855 (Out-of-state)
Products: Jewelry displayers; risers

Edwin Freed Inc.
151 W. 46th St.
New York, NY 10036
212-391-2170
Products: Jewelry pads; displayers; case liners; pricing kits

File-A-Gem
Box 539
Baxter Springs, KS 66713
316-856-3800
Product: Loose gemstone file holders

Graves Co.
1800 Andrews Ave., Ext. North
Pompano Beach, FL 33069
305-960-0300
800-327-9103 (Out-of-state)
Product: Gemstone holders

Los Angeles Window Display Co.
536 Towne Ave.
Los Angeles, CA 90013
213-624-3613
Products: Jewelry displayers; risers; case liners; fabric

**Presentation Box
Div. of Int'l. Packaging Corp.**
517 Mineral Spring Ave.
Pawtucket, RI 02862
401-724-1600
800-556-7390 (Out-of-state)
Products: Jewelry displayers; slot wall; soft suede (54 inches)

Princess Tanya Inc.
8255 Firestone Blvd., Ste. 501
Downey, CA 90241
213-869-8809
Products: Jewelry displayers; risers; boxes

Rocket Jewelry Box
125 E. 144th St.
Bronx, NY 10451
212-292-5370
Product: Jewelry boxes (display and gift)

Fabric

Coral of Chicago
2001 S. Calumet Ave.
Chicago, IL 60616
312-225-5800
800-621-5250
Product: Fabric

Dazian Fabrics
423 W. 55th St.
New York, NY 10019
212-307-7800
Product: Fabric

Los Angeles Window Display Co.
536 Towne Ave.
Los Angeles, CA 90013
213-624-3613
Products: Velvet; soft suede (48 inches); ultrasuede

**Presentation Box
  Div. of Int'l. Packaging Corp.**
517 Mineral Spring Ave.
Pawtucket, RI 02862
401-724-1600
800-556-7390 (Out-of-state)
Products: Soft suede (54 inches); velvet; ultrasuede

Signage & Graphics

Ad-Mart Inc.
Gose Pike & Stanford Rd.
Danville, KY 40422
606-236-7600
800-354-2102 (Out-of-state)
Product: Display letters

Big Apple Signs
31 W. 46th St.
New York, NY 10036
212-772-0726
800-237-5052
Products: Letters; logos

Central Sales Promotions, Inc.
130 NE 50th St. (73105)
P.O. Box 53444
Oklahoma City, OK 73152
405-525-2335
800-654-8435 (Out-of-state)
Products: Window & showcase signs; pricing kits

Clearr Corp.
150 W. 60th St.
Minneapolis, MN 55419
612-866-3478
800-548-3269 (Out-of-state)
Product: Lightboxes

Color 2000, Inc.
P.O. Box 11323
570 Jessie St.
San Francisco, CA 94101
415-861-5151
Products: Photos & transparencies

Custom Color Lab
940 Commercial St.
Palo Alto, CA 94303
415-494-7761
Products: Photos & transparencies

DSA/Phototech, Inc.
3383 Livonia Ave.
Los Angeles, CA 90034
213-559-9870
800-327-3723 (Out-of-state)
Product: Lightboxes

Display Concepts, Inc.
P.O. Box 175
Bar Harbor, ME 04609
207-667-3386
800-446-0033 (Out-of-state)
Product: Display letters

Electra Letters
90 Remington Blvd.
Ronkonkoma, NY 11779
516-585-5659
800-247-7420 (In-state)
Product: Display letters

Filmet Color Labs
7436 Washington St.
Pittsburgh, PA 15218
412-351-3510
800-222-1223
Products: Photos & transparencies

Gamma Technologies, Inc.
12255 SW 132nd Ct.
Miami, FL 33186
305-251-5775
800-522-7446 (Out-of-state)
Products: Photos & transparencies

Letter Craft Inc.
280 Midland Ave., Bldg. M
Saddle Brock, NJ 07662
201-794-3630
Products: Display letters logos; graphics; sign holders (acrylic)

Lettersigns Inc.
801 Main St.
Stone Mountain, GA 30083
404-498-0583
800-438-2685 (Out-of-state)
Products: Display letters; logos

Meisel Commercial Photographic
96-45 Webbs Chapel Rd.
Dallas, TX 75220
214-350-6666
800-827-5186 (Out-of-state)
Products: Photos & transparencies

Meteor Photo Co.
1099 Chicago Rd.
Troy, MI 48007-3301
313-583-3090
800-521-4790 (Out-of-state)
Products: Photos & transparencies

Polyplastic Forms, Inc.
49 Gazza Blvd.
Farmingdale, NY 11735
516-249-5011
Products: Display letters; graphics

Scott Plastics Co.
P.O. Box 1047
Tallevast, FL 34270
813-355-5171
800-237-9447 (Out-of-state)
Products: Display letters; pricing kits

Trans Lights, Inc.
2300 Marilyn Ln.
Columbus, OH 43219
614-471-1685
Product: Lightboxes

Van Pelt Photographer
752 N. Seward St.
Los Angeles, CA 90038
213-462-6604
Products: Gem posters; gem birthday book; gem photography

Lighting

Alkco Lighting Co.
11500 Melrose Ave.
Franklin Park, IL 60131
312-451-0700
Product: Accent lighting

Amerlux
23 Daniel Rd.
Fairfield, NJ 07006
201-882-8298
Product: Low-voltage fixtures

Capri Lighting
6430 E. Slauson Ave.
Los Angeles, CA 90040
213-726-1800
Product: Low-voltage fixtures

Columbia Lighting Co.
N. 3808 Sullivan Rd.
Spokane, WA 99216
509-924-7000
Product: Fluorescent fixtures

Danalite
16392 Gothard St., Unit A
Huntington Beach, CA 92647
714-841-4325
Products: Showcase 12-volt, high-intensity halogen strip and lamps; accent lighting

ESV Inc.
525 Court St.
Pekin, IL 61554
309-347-6685
800-423-6411
Product: Accent lighting

Econo-lite Products Inc.
316 Princeton Ave.
Jersey City, NJ 07305
201-434-6853
800-345-9652 (Out-of-state)
Products: 20-watt, quartz-halogen showcase lights; accent lighting

Farralane Ent., Inc.
166 Central Ave.
Farmingdale, NY 11747
516-752-9824
800-433-7057 (Out-of-state)
Product: Special effects lighting

GTE Sylvania — U.S. Lighting Div.
100 Endicott St.
Danvers, MA 01923
617-777-1900
Products: Low-voltage MR16 lamps; fluorescent lamps

General Electric Lighting
Nela Park
Cleveland, OH 44112
216-266-3200
Products: Low-voltage MR16 lamps; fluorescent lamps

Grand & Benedicts
1 SE Second Ave.
Portland, OR 97214
503-232-3869
800-452-9385 (In-state)
800-367-8352 (Out-of-state)
Product: Accent lighting

Inlite Corp.
939 Grayson St.
Berkeley, CA 94710
415-849-1067
Product: Accent lighting

Lazin Lighting, Inc.
53 Greene St., 5th Fl.
New York, NY 10013
212-219-3888
Product: Accent lighting

Lighting Services Inc.
Industrial Park, Rt. 9W
Stony Point, NY 10980
914-942-2800
Products: Low-voltage fluorescent fixtures; accent lighting

Lightolier, Inc.
100 Lighting Way
Secaucus, NJ 07094
201-392-3903
Products: Low-voltage fluorescent fixtures

Lithonia Lighting
P.O. Box A
Conyers, GA 30207
404-922-9000
Products: Low-voltage fluorescent fixtures

North American Philips Lighting Corp.
Philips Square
CN 6800
Somerset, NJ 08873
800-631-1259
Product: General & accent lighting

Precision Industries
512-SE 32nd St.
Ft. Lauderdale, FL 33316
305-522-3738
Product: Special effects lighting

Roxter Mfg. Corp.
10-11 40th Ave.
Long Island City, NY 11101
718-392-5060
Product: Accent lighting

Staff Lighting Corp.
Rt. 9W
Highland, NY 12528
914-691-6262
Product: Accent lighting

Times Square Lighting
318 W. 47th St.
New York, NY 10036
212-245-4155
Product: Accent lighting

VL Service Lighting
108 S. Franklin Ave., Ste. 9
Valley Stream, NY 11582
212-285-9364
Product: Criticolor fluorescent lamps for grading stones

Venture Lighting International
625 Golden Oak Pkwy.
Cleveland, OH 44146
216-232-5970
800-437-0111 (Out-of-state)
Products: MR16 low-voltage lamps with dichroic reflector, excellent beam control

Materials

Advanced Technology, Inc.
311 Regional Rd., S.
Greensboro, NC 27409
919-668-0488
800-632-1320 (Out-of-state)
Product: Laminates

Cameron Glass, Inc.
P.O. Box 471500
Tulsa, OK 74147
918-252-9546
800-331-3666 (Out-of-state)
Product: Showcase & shelving glass

Consolidated Glass Corp.
P.O. Box 430
New Castle, PA 16103
412-658-4541
Product: Showcase & shelving glass

Elgin Precision Glass
1200 Abbot Dr.
Elgin, IL 60123
312-931-1200
Product: Showcase & shelving glass

Formica Corp.
155 Rt. 46W
Wayne, NJ 07470-0980
800-624-1914 (In-state)
800-524-0159 (Out-of-state)
Product: Laminates

Harwood Protection Industries Inc.
8580 Cinderbed Rd., Ste. 1200
Newington, VA 22122
800-852-8577
Product: Security glass

Interlam
400 SE 12th St., Bldg. E
Ft. Lauderdale, FL 33316
305-764-7855
800-237-7052 (Out-of-state)
Product: Laminates

Laminated Glass Corp.
375 Church Ave.
Telfor, PA 18969
215-721-0400
Product: Security glass

Libby Owens Ford Co.
P.O. Box 799
811 Madison Ave.
Toledo, OH 43695
419-247-3731
Product: Security glass

Nevamar Corp.
8339 Telegraph Rd.
Odenton, MD 21113
800-233-9485 (In-state)
800-638-4380 (Out-of-state)
Product: Laminates

PPG Industries, Inc.
One PPG Place
Pittsburgh, PA 15272
412-434-3131
Product: Window glass

Ram Products
1111 N. Centerville Rd.
Sturgis, MI 49091
616-651-9351
800-253-2064 (Out-of-state)
Product: Laminates

Wilsonart
P.O. Box 6110 (76503-6110)
600 General Bruce Dr.
Temple, TX 76504
817-778-2711
800-792-6000 (In-state)
800-433-3222 (Out-of-state)
Product: Laminates

Winona Industries Inc.
602 E. Front St.
Winona, MN 55987
507-454-1860
800-826-2687 (In-state)
Product: Laminates

Miscellaneous

Cactus Mat Mfg. Co.
4131 Arden Dr.
El Monte, CA 91731
213-283-0587
Products: Benches & stools

George Dell, Inc.
151 W. 25th St.
New York, NY 10001
212-206-8460
Product: Display props

Charlotte Co.
24241 Cataluna Circle
Mission Viejo, CA 92691
213-617-1134
Products: Showcase stools & claiborne benches

Otema Store Fixtures Ltd.
101 Don Park Rd.
Markham, ON L6W 2J2
CANADA
416-475-1066
Product: Showcase stools

Rainwater Diamond & Gold Warehouse
Box 799
Rt. 2, Flagcrest Plaza
Trinity, AL 35673
205-351-7722
Product: Monthly promotional programs

Worden Co.
199 E. 17th St.
Holland, MI 49423
616-392-1848
Product: Showcase stools

index

a

Advertising message, 31, 36
 for promotions, 54
Analogous hues, 54
Asymmetrical composition, 5
Awnings, 36

b

Birthstones, 45

c

Christmas, 56, 59—62
Cleaning jewelry, 50
Cleaning window, 51
Color
 cool, 10
 complementary, 10, 12—13
 diamonds and, 64—65
 lights and, 20
 primary, 9
 schemes, 13—14
 spectrum, 9
 symbolic meanings of, 14—15
 trends, researching, 12
 used for selling, 9—15
 warm, 9
 wheel, 9
Composition of displays, 3—8
Constructing interior windows, 38
Construction work, contracting, 75
Courtesy cards, 43
Customers, targeting, 48, 53, 74

d

Diamonds
 colors for displaying, 64—65
 displaying, 63—66
 lighting for, 21, 65
Display, of volume-produced items, 5
Displayers (see "Presentation displayers")
Display units
 proportions of, 6
 space between, 8

e

Employees, 55

f

Fashion
 and jewelry, 15, 31
 as source of ideas, 42
Fashion magazines, ideas from, 56
Female-oriented windows, 32
Floor, for window interiors, 38—40
Focal points, 5

h

Heat-sensitive gems, lighting for, 22
Heat, venting from windows, 37
Height point, 6

i

Increasing sales, by pricing items, 36
Insurance, 55, 76, 79, 80
Intermediate hues, 10
Intermediate position, 6

l

Laws, signs and local, 36
Lease rate, 37
Lettering, for show cards, 34—35
Lighting,
 cool, 20
 for customer viewing, 18—20
 for display area, 17
 down light, 21
 in large store, 18
 to overcome reflections, 20
 plans for, 18—20
 selecting colors for, 20
 for showcase interiors, 23
 suspended, 18
 track, 20
 warm, 20

m

Male-oriented windows, 32
Malls, security in, 80
Manufacturers' representatives, 69
Media, at promotions, 53
Merchandise
 selecting, 50
 size of, 49
Monotone settings, 13
Mood-elevating rooms, 18

n

Name brands, 69

p

Pins, displaying, 28
Photographing windows, 84
 preventing reflections while, 86
Planning
 merchandise, 74
 outline for, 74—75
 space, 74
 for store interior, 75
 to target audience, 74
 for window displays, 48—51
Presentation displayers
 imaginative, 29
 size of, 25
 types of, 27—28
Pricing items, 36
Primary colors, 9
Props, 43
 free of charge, 43, 55
Promotions
 advertising for, 54
 determining purpose for, 53
 frequency of, 54
 planning, 54
 reducing expense of, 55
 themes for, 56—57

s

Safes, 79
Sale windows, 48
Seasonal display themes, 43
 window changes and, 15
Secondary colors, 10
Security, 38, 51, 55, 62, 76, 79—81
Security glass, 38
Setting up windows, 51
Shades of color, 12
Show cards, 31
 lettering, 35
 preparing, 50
 researching design for, 34
Showcase interiors, lighting for, 23
Signage, 31—36
 awnings used as, 36
Split complements, 14
Standard voltage lamps, 20
Steel screens, 38

Store interior, planning, 75
Subordinate position, 6
Symbolic meanings of colors, 14
Symmetrical composition, 5

t

Television, closed-circuit, 79
Themes
    anniversary, 44—45
    cultural, 43
    historical, 44
    holiday, 44—45, 60
    for promotions, 56—57
    seasonal, 43
Tints, 12
Tones, 12
Transformers, 21—23
Triadic harmony, 14
Triangular composition, 5—7

v

Visual task, 18—20

w

Walls, for window interiors, 38
Warm colors (see "Colors")
Watches, displaying, 67—70
Wedding anniversaries, gifts, 45
Windows, 37—40
    constructing interiors for, 38
    drawing layout of, 49—50
    height point of, 6
    ideal proportions for, 25, 37
    lighting systems and, 37
    setting up, 51
    themes for (see "Themes")
    venting heat from, 37
    walls for, 38